WASHINGTON ON $10 MILLION A DAY

HOW LOBBYISTS PLUNDER THE NATION

KEN SILVERSTEIN

COMMON COURAGE PRESS   MONROE, MAINE

For Sophia and, as always, Clara

Library of Congress Cataloging-in Publication Data
Silverstein, Ken.
   Washington on $10 million a day: how lobbyists plunder the nation
/Ken Silverstein
p.   cm
Includes index.
ISBN 1-56751-137-6 (hardcover)
1. Lobbying--United States. 2. Lobbyists--United States.
3. Political participation--United States.
I. Title

JK1118.S575 1998   98-9483
324'.4'0973--dc21   CIP

Common Courage Press
Box 702
Monroe, ME 04951

207-525-0900 fax: 207-525-3068
e-mail: comcour@agate.net
http://www.agate.net/~comcour
First Printing

CONTENTS

ACKNOWLEDGMENTS

Thanks to Greg Bates of Common Courage, who told me he'd publish any book I wanted to write for him and has been generous in his support for this one. Ben Sonnenberg helped me with the title for the book and John Stauber provided the title for the Introduction. I shamelessly stole the title for Chapter 4 from a wonderful article Art Levine wrote for *Spy* magazine a few years ago. Thanks to Jeffrey St. Clair for allowing me to adapt an article we co-authored about Al Gore's stable of lobbyists/fundraisers. Thanks to John Richards of the Center for the Study of Responsive Law for his support.

Most of this book is comprised of my own original research and investigation. Parts of it have been published in *CounterPunch, Mother Jones, Harper's, The Nation, The Progressive, The Village Voice, In These Times* and *Multinational Monitor*. I also relied on reports in a number of magazines and newspapers, especially Washington publications such as *Roll Call, The Hill, Legal Times* and *National Journal*.

Readers wishing to contact me can write me at *CounterPunch*, an investigative newsletter I co-edit from Washington (Subscriptions for 1 year, 22 issues: $40/$25 low-income and students). The address is *CounterPunch*, P.O. Box 18675, Washington, DC 20036.

Ken Silverstein
Washington, D.C.
January 1998

INTRODUCTION

PIMPS TO POWER

Lobbyists and the
Destruction of Democracy

When *Fortune* published its 1997 list of the nation's top 500 corporations, the magazine could barely restrain its exuberance. The previous year had been "extraordinary" with regard to profitability, *Fortune* said, as companies "restructured, reengineered, refinanced, downsized, laid off, split up, and merged their way to prosperity." All this had been furthered by "an almost magically favorable economic climate," highlighted by low interest rates and "benign labor costs."

For business and the wealthy, these past few years truly have been the best of times. Profits at Fortune 500 firms rose by 23.3 percent in 1997, after climbing by 13.4 percent the previous year. Salaries for top managers are also soaring. *Business Week*, a publication not normally known for its radical politics, says executive pay is "Out of Control." The magazine reports that the average salary and bonus for CEOs at the nation's biggest firms rose by 39 percent in 1996, to $2.3 million. Total compensation, which includes retirement benefits, incentive plans and stock option packages, was up 54 percent, to $5.7 million. Corporate America's hired help didn't do nearly as well. Workers' salaries rose about 3 percent in 1996, leaving average compensation for CEOs at 209 times higher than that of factory workers.

Meanwhile, the wealthy are paying less and less to the treasury in the form of taxes. Some 2,400 Americans with annual income of $200,000 or more paid no taxes in 1993, compared to just 85 wealthy individuals who escaped paying taxes in 1977. Since Congress in 1997 reduced inheritance taxes and the tax on capital gains, the number of rich Americans who pay little or no taxes is expected to grow in coming years.

Corporations are also avoiding tax payments. Two loopholes Congress provided to companies with operations overseas—the foreign tax credit and tax deferral on foreign income—cost the treasury about $24 billion per year. The bland term "accelerated depreciation" obscures a rule that allows companies to write off the cost of equipment faster than it actually wears out, a gift worth $28.3 billion annually. Overall, federal corporate income taxes have declined from 30.1 percent of total tax revenues during the 1940s to 12.2 percent in 1996.

Huge corporate profits and low taxes for the wealthy do indeed result from a "favorable economic climate," but there's nothing magical about it, as *Fortune* would have you believe. The policies behind the favorable climate are designed by politicians who are dependent on cash from Corporate America to finance their political careers. The deluge of business dollars—in 1996, the parties and their candidates raised $2.1 billion, an average of $5.75 million every day—means that elected leaders are sure to implement policies designed to fatten their sponsors' bottom lines.

The link between campaign donations and political policy was brought into sharp focus by the campaign finance scandals that erupted during the 1996 campaign. Even jaded observers were startled by the Clinton administration's selling of the Lincoln bedroom to the highest bidder, and its organizing of White House coffee klatsches to reward donors and encourage them to make additional contributions.

But political contributions are only one way that big business wins favors in Washington. The media's focus on who made what phone calls from where, and who gave what funds in exchange for which favors misses a broader picture. Understanding how the capital works, and how business prospers here, requires a trip through the world of beltway lobbying and a review of the vast army of hired guns working at the behest of Corporate America.

Dollar for dollar, lobbying is a better investment than campaign contributions, one reason business spends far more on the former than on the latter. In 1996, Philip Morris coughed up $19.6 million for lobbying programs versus $4.2 million for campaign donations (making it the leader in both categories). The same pattern holds true with other firms. For 1996, Georgia Pacific spent $8.9 million for lobbying and handed out $527,000 in political money. Corresponding figures for AT&T are $8.4 million versus $1.8 million; for Pfizer, $8.3 million versus $775,000; for Boeing, $5.2 million versus $770,000; for ARCO, $4.3 million versus $1.4 million; for Lockheed, $3.5 million versus $1.26 million; for Fedex, $3.1 million versus $1.9 million; for Dow Chemical $1.5 million versus $578,000.

In addition to in-house efforts, most big corporations spend lavishly for outside lobbying firms. Lockheed, for example, retains at least two dozen beltway lobby shops to supplement its own efforts, while Fedex has an additional 10 firms on retainer. In 1996, Boeing hired seven outside lobby shops for the sole purpose of pushing renewed Most Favored Nation trade status for China, paying them a combined total of at least $160,000 for their efforts.

While corporate lobbying has long been a major force in American politics, it has also been greatly transformed during the past few decades. Today, many efforts involve stealth lobbying—the chief tactic here is mobilizing fake "grassroots" campaigns—or with indirect methods, such as buying research from friendly think tanks in order to influence Congress and public opinion. All of this makes calculating corporate lobbying expenditures nearly impossible, though it's safe to say that lobbying has now become a multi-billion dollar-per-year industry. No one can say whether the figure of $10 million dollars a day in this book's title is accurate. But the trend would suggest it will soon be a very significant understatement—even if weekends and holidays are included.

When you consider the enormous benefits bestowed on Corporate America by the White House and Congress, the big sums companies spend to win favors are revealed as chump change. Lockheed's combined expenditures on lobbying and campaign contributions were about $5 million in 1996. That same year, Lockheed's lobbyists, with help from other arms makers, won approval for the creation of a new $15 billion government fund that will underwrite foreign weapon sales. In 1996, Microsoft spent less than $2 million for its combined lobbying and campaign contribution expenditures (the former accounted for more than two-thirds of that amount). The following year Congress awarded the company tax credits worth hundreds of millions of dollars for the sale of licenses to manufacture its software programs overseas.

Corporate lobbyists don't win every battle (though when they lose it's often because a competing corporate faction bought up even more lobbying firepower). It is indisputable, though, that corporate citizens who retain lobbyists have an enormous advantage in Washington over the regular ones who merely vote. Tommy Boggs, perhaps Washington's best known influence peddler, charges $550 per hour for his services. That's a drop in the bucket to Philip Morris, but Boggs' rate would eat up the average salary earner's entire annual income after a mere 43 hours of lobbying activity.

That lobbying has corrupted the political system is no secret. During his 1992 presidential campaign, Bill Clinton promised to "break the stranglehold the special interests have on our elections and the lobbyists have on our government." Such promises (like many others the president made) were forgotten as soon as the election votes were counted. Clinton picked Vernon Jordan, a top lobbyist and one of Washington's consummate political insiders, to head his presidential transition team. Among those selected for top administration jobs were Ron Brown, a former colleague of Tommy Boggs at the firm of Patton Boggs; Mickey Kantor of the powerhouse firm Manatt, Phelps, & Phillips; and Howard Paster, a former lobbyist for oil companies, banks and weapons makers.

A more recent display of the administration's open door policy to lobbyists came with the White House coffee klatsches. Examine the list of the roughly 1,500 people who attended the affairs and one finds that lobbyists were among the most heavily represented.

Republicans criticize Clinton for his coziness with special interests, but they maintain the same intimate relationships with corporate lobbyists. After winning control of Congress in 1994, the GOP House leadership met weekly with "The Thursday Group," a pack of lobbyists and activists who helped plot legislative and media strategy on the Contract With America. Included in this elite troupe were hired guns representing the U.S. Chamber of Commerce, the National Federation of Independent Business, and Americans for Tax Reform.

Washington on Ten Million Dollars A Day tells how monied interests use lobbyists to achieve their goals in Washington, and why no one in the capital seems to want to do anything to change the system. It's also about the woeful ethical standards of Washington lobbyists, most whom will represent any client, from a corporate criminal to a foreign despot, as long as the bills get paid on time.

Fundamentally, though, *Washington on Ten Million Dollars A Day* is about corporate power and the destruction of American democracy. Though the historic vibrancy of this country's democratic system has been vastly inflated by historians and official myth makers, there was a time when the average citizen could make his or her voice heard in the capital. Today, the vast lobbying power of corporations and the wealthy has reduced the collective voice of average citizens to a faint din, barely heard in the corridors of power.

This state of affairs is amply reflected by the political process. Back in 1993, the hottest political issue in Washington was health care. President Clinton called the American system the "costliest and most wasteful" in the world and promised that when he was through, the American people would be able to stand tall and say, "Your government has the courage, finally, to take on the health care profiteers and make health care affordable for every family."

The public would have enthusiastically supported a frontal assault on the health care industry, with polls showing Canada's socialized system being the most popular model for reform. The public, though, was largely excluded from the debate in Washington, which was dominated by the "health care profiteers" that Clinton had pledged to attack. A report from the Center for Public Integrity found that some 660 groups shelled out more than $100 million to thwart reform between 1993 and 1994. About one-quarter of that amount took the form of political donations to members of Congress. A good chunk of the rest was paid to hundreds of lobbying and public relations firms that were hired to influence the health care debate.

At least 80 lobbyists working the issue were former members of Congress or the executive branch. William Gradison was a member of Congress on Sunday and head of the Health Insurers Association of America (HIAA)—a trade group of 270 insurance companies and creator of the infamous "Harry and Louise" TV ads—on Monday. The beltway firm Powell

Tate was hired by Bristol-Myers Squibb, RJR Nabisco, T2 Medical Inc.,Pharmacia & Upjohn, and Searle. For $2 million, according to an internal memorandum, Powell Tate would "sow doubt" about Clinton's assaults on drug makers and his early calls for price controls on the industry.

The National Federation of Independent Business, one of Washington's most powerful groups with more than 600,000 small business affiliates spread across every congressional district, launched a huge effort to defeat any plan that required employers to help pay for their workers' health care. Over two years, the federation generated two million letters opposing reform and maintained a crew of 10 lobbyists working full time on the issue. "Our structure is very similar to the White House," Federation chieftain John Motley bragged to the Center. "Actually, I've got more people working in the House [of Representatives] than they do...I think they have about four. I've got six."

Consumer and public interest groups also lobbied on health care, but they did not have anywhere near the resources of the business interests. Even Gradison admitted that some groups weren't "well represented" in the debate, saying, "I don't mean there are zero advocates but there aren't a lot of advocates for the poor."

Since average citizens—including nearly 40 million Americans without health care coverage—were not heard from, talk of comprehensive health care reform soon faded. The general public's minuscule influence on political affairs was seen in the fact that a Canadian-style system, while being the single most popular plan with the populace, was swiftly discarded by Clinton and Congress because, said the pundits, it suffered from a lack of political support!

The same divide between public opinion and political power can be seen across the board. People earning less than $22,600 a year outnumber people earning more than $246,000 per year by 40 to 1, but in 1997 Congress passed a plan that reduced the average tax payment for those in the latter category by $16,000, while increasing annual taxes for those in the former by $19. With the end of the Cold War, most Americans hoped for a "peace dividend" in the form of reduced spending for the military and more money for social programs. Yet year after year, Congress and the White House continue to lard the Pentagon with hundreds of billions of dollars while cutting social expenditures to the bone. Welfare programs have been eliminated so that Cold War relics such as Northrop's B-2 bomber can be preserved.

Such outcomes are predictable given the overwhelming influence exerted on the political system by Corporate America's hired guns. Indeed, the American political system is now presided over by lobbyists: they organize fundraisers and otherwise keep lawmakers supplied with campaign cash. They open doors for clients at the White House and government agencies. Because many formerly served in government, they know the rules and how to bend them.

Washington on Ten Million Dollars A Day will tell you—and show you—how lobbyists have bought up the capital and give you the information you need to fight back.

CHAPTER ONE

THEIR MASTERS' VOICE

Meet America's
Unelected Branch of Government

"The locus of decision-making in the political process is
rapidly shifting from politicians and civil servants to lobbyists."
—Peter Drucker, *The New Realities*

What do lobbyists do and how do they do it? When I set out
to write a book about Washington lobbying in the spring of
1997, I wanted to explore those questions with an inside look.
My ability to get an inside look, though, did not appear to be
promising. I'm rarely invited to functions attended by lobbyists
or other beltway power brokers, and felt awkward even asking
for interviews since I've written numerous magazine articles
critical of the influence peddling occupation. Anyone with
access to the Internet or a newspaper database could swiftly
determine that my aim, from the profession's point of view, was
not admirable.

Hence, I decided to pose as a Washington influence peddler
eager to contribute to political candidates. I created a fictitious
Political Action Committee affiliated with the equally fictitious Miami-based United Broadcasting Corporation. Armed
with my impressive credentials as a lobbyist for this cash-dis-
pensing outfit, I called the offices of Democratic and
Republican Party fundraising outfits and asked for information
about upcoming affairs in Washington.

I was initially nervous about making the calls. At the time, both parties were under fire for having deployed shady fundraising tactics during the 1996 campaign and it seemed likely that party operatives would make at least superficial inquiries about unknown donors. If I got past that point, I feared being swiftly unmasked as a fraud if party staffers asked any detailed questions about my company's operations.

I need not have worried. After I provided a minimal amount of background information, staffers from both parties eagerly sent me material and urged me to call anytime if I needed further assistance. No one asked troublesome questions; they were too busy trying to get me on board as a new contributor.

The National Republican Congressional Committee (NRCC)—whose list of events is "blast faxed" to PAC directors, lobbyists and other high rollers every Friday—provided me with information about 44 fund-raisers. These included a Defense Aerospace Industry Dinner for Congressman Chris Cannon of Utah ($500); an Indy 500 Warm-Up Reception for Dan Burton at the American Trucking Association ($500); and a Happy Birthday Speaker Newt Gingrich Reception at the Capitol Hill Club ($1,000). That the two political parties share all too similar interests was reflected in the fact that several GOP fund-raisers were to be held at the lobby shop of Dan Dutko, a diehard Democrat and intimate of Vice President Al Gore.

Though I called only to ask about events for individual members of Congress, NRCC staffer Robert Eppihimer suggested that I also talk to someone who handles party fund-raising. "PAC or 'soft'?," he inquired, voice aquiver, before forwarding me to Anne Ekern at the National Republican Senatorial Committee (NRSC). Ekern, too, wanted to know if United Broadcasting would be making PAC or more highly prized soft money donations. When I pleaded ignorance, saying I was still a bit new to the field, she replied, "Don't worry, we'll get you educated."

Ekern told me that for $5,000 in PAC money, United Broadcasting could join the Republican Senate Council. That would entitle my firm to send a representative to a monthly luncheon where a GOP Senator would brief participants, mostly corporate lobbyists, on "legislation on anything else that might be going through [Congress]." If United Broadcasting preferred to pony up $25,000 in soft money, the company could join the Chairman's Foundation which, Ekern said, "catered to the CEO." Members of the Foundation are invited to attend four or five small dinners annually featuring Senators and senior committee staffers, and also take part in four major NRSC meetings a year.

Soon after my conversation with Ekern I received an invitation from Senate majority leader Trent Lott to attend a "policy forum" that promised "plenty of opportunities to share your personal ideas and visions" with Lott, Senate Finance Committee chairman William Roth and Budget Committee chairman Pete Domenici. (At roughly the same time, Lott had signed his name to a direct mail pitch addressed to people wanting to "stop Bill Clinton from pursuing the radical liberal agenda of big labor and the special interests who financed his re-election campaign." To achieve this goal Lott recommended that "patriotic Americans" send the Republican Party $25 to $100 or more.)

The Democratic Congressional Campaign Committee was equally helpful, providing a list of 24 fund-raisers. These included a reception for Minority Leader Richard Gephardt at the Naval Heritage Center—tickets cost between $1,000 and $5,000—and a golf tournament and dinner hosted by Congressman Nick Rahall of West Virginia, offered at the bargain basement rate of $500 for PACs and $150 for individuals.

The DCCC's Erin Graefe also sent me information about

the Committee's donor programs. Fifteen thousand dollars in PAC money will buy you a seat in the Speaker's Club. Annual benefits include "bimonthly issue and political briefings with administration members," "small dinners" with ranking members of Congress, and invitations to a Colorado ski trip in January, a winter retreat in March and a Washington area golf tournament in May, all with Democratic officials and elected leaders. Those who paid up by March 1 were to receive a bonus invitation to the Wintergreen Golf Tournament, the Skeet and Trap Shoot, the Arizona Golf Tournament, or a summer retreat in Newport, Rhode Island.

A colleague of Graefe's soon faxed me an invitation to the Democratic Senatorial Campaign Committee's (DSCC) upcoming "Taste of the States" affair, where for $5,000 per couple participants could sample regional cuisine from around the country and mingle with Senate minority leader Tom Daschle and other prominent Democrats. [Meanwhile, the DSCC's head, Senator Bob Kerrey of Nebraska, was sending out a direct mail pitch to people "fed up with the current campaign finance system that allows big money special interests to push your interest aside." To combat the "tidal wave of big money," Kerrey urged recipients to: (1) contact Senate majority leader Lott to demand an end to "Republican gridlock on campaign finance reform"; and (2) send the D.S.C.C a contribution of anywhere from $35 to $500.]

My Life as a Bagman

I couldn't afford to attend any of the big money affairs, but I did buy tickets to two individual fund-raisers. The first was a $500 per person event to benefit second-term Congressman George Radanovich (R) of California. The affair—dubbed a "Wine Reception," presumably because Radanovich is one of Congress's two wine growers as well as a shill for the alcohol industry—was held at the offices of McClure, Gerard & Neuenschwander, a leading beltway lobby shop. The company

Rep. George Radanovich: Mr. Booze Goes to Washington. A winemaker, Radanovich has found his chief mission as shill for the alcohol industry and agricultural interests.

was founded by former Idaho Senator James McClure and represents a host of energy and mining companies, including the National Mining Association.

The site was well chosen as Radanovich is a leading practitioner of environmental rape-and-pillage, with his campaigns generously funded by logging, oil and waste disposal companies (as well as by McClure's client, the NMA). The congressman also works hard for agricultural interests, which poured $76,808 into his campaign war chest. All told, Radanovich raised $410,000 for his 1996 re-election bid. Not a huge amount by current standards, but bear in mind that his opponent, Paul Barile, spent only $5,340.

I arrived a few minutes early for the 5:30 affair and was so nervous that I circled the block for 15 minutes, mentally rehearsing what I imagined to be suave power broker chit chat, while waiting for people to arrive. When I finally mustered my courage and made my entrance, no one was on hand but a few of Radanovich's staffers and several lobbyists from McClure's firm. Among the latter group was Joe Findaro, who'd worked for James Watt, Reagan's famously rabid Interior Department chieftain. It was Findaro who greeted Radanovich when he turned up a few minutes later, saying, his arms sweeping the room, "*Mi casa es su casa.*"

Soon, the reception area was filled with about 30 people, most of them lobbyists for big business: Enron, Sunkist, the National Roofing Contractors Association, and BHP, an Australian-owned mining and oil company. With the exception of myself, guests seemed to be well acquainted, and each new arrival brought a tide of boisterous welcomes. People chatted around tables amply stocked with food—quesadillas, curried chicken skewers, stuffed mushrooms—and an assortment of wines from Radanovich's vineyards.

The wine was served by the Congressman's chief of staff, John McMamman, who also received envelopes stuffed with checks. As he filled my glass with a tasty Merlot, McMamman accepted an envelope from Ed Bedwell of Pacific Gas & Electric, who said that his offering contained checks from several colleagues as well. Tribute passed, Bedwell was soon immersed in a lengthy discussion with Radanovich about utility issues.

Meanwhile, two Washington old-timers—Bob Schramm, now a lobbyist for California agribusiness, and Miles Dwyer, a Capitol Hill fixture since the L.B.J. days—exchanged stories. As he nibbled hors d'oeuvres, Schramm recalled how in the early 1970s, Charles Colson, then Nixon's special counsel, didn't even answer a letter Schramm wrote to seek an endorsement for a friend who was running for office. "When someone

I know calls me looking for help, I'm there for them," Schramm said bitterly.

"That's what this town's built on," replied Dwyer.

Though the phone calls to party fund-raising units had proved easy, mingling with this high-powered crowd made me edgy. I rigorously avoided any lengthy discussions, hoping to avoid having to explain why a Florida-based media company would want to attend a fund-raiser for a California congressmen who specializes in agricultural issues. I also feared that my frequent dashes to the bathroom—where I could discreetly take notes in a stall—might raise suspicions, or at least concern that I had been stricken with a life-threatening intestinal ailment.

Once again my worries were groundless. In fact, Radanovich's staffers insisted that I meet the guest of honor, who enthusiastically thanked me for coming. When I asked his staffer Lisa Ford about the possibility of setting up a future meeting between the Congressman and United Broadcasting officials, she said, "Oh definitely. I usually know where he's at, so just give me a call."

Exit Tweedledee, Enter Tweedledum

On the night following the Radanovich affair I attended a $500 per person fund-raiser for Texas Democrat Ken Bentsen at The Monocle, a popular haunt of politicians and lobbyists. While Bentsen held court in the restaurant's Federal Room South, Senator Tim Johnson of South Dakota was collecting money across the hall in Federal Room North.

Bentsen is a prodigious fund-raiser, spending $1.4 million in 1996 to fend off his Republican challenger, Dolly Madison McKenna. Of that amount, $905,000 came from PACs, with labor providing $364,000, the biggest chunk. Like his uncle, former treasury secretary and senator Lloyd Bentsen, Ken is a close ally of the oil industry, and his support elicited a geyser of $32,214 from energy and natural resource companies for the congressman's 1996 campaign. Other big financial supporters of Bentsen's include lawyers and lobbyists ($58,000) and bankers ($79,000).

This donor base was well reflected by the crowd of about forty at The Monocle. Labor was represented by the Teamsters, the United Auto Workers and the United Food and Commercial Workers. Finance money came in the form of Goldman, Sachs & Co., Citicorp and the National Association of Mortgage Brokers. Oil and energy contributors included Shell and Enron. Lobbyists came from such venerable firms as Akin, Gump, Strauss, Hauer & Feld and McDermott, Will & Emery.

As at the previous night's gathering, guests huddled to exchange war stories. Two finance sector lobbyists traded tips about helpful staffers on Congressional committees, while other influence peddlers talked legislative and political strategy with Bentsen and several other members of Congress who turned up, including Representatives Zoe Lofgren of California, Chet Edwards of Texas and John Dingell of Michigan. Steve Verdier of America's Community Bankers explained to Debbie Dingell, John's wife, that his group was wary about prodding Congress too hard since "we pretty much got what we wanted" last term.

Having had no problems the previous night, I confidently talked with Bentsen's staffers and others in attendance (though I again worried that guests might be alarmed by my constant sprints for the restroom). Brenda O'Lenick, Bentsen's executive assistant, explained to me that fundraising events tend to attract the same people because the pool of donors—"other than small contributors who really believe in the candidate"—is tiny. "It's mostly lobbyists," she said. "Some attend three of these a night. They have to stick with ginger ale, otherwise they might end up in trouble. Some of them don't come at all; they just send along a check."

Jerry Woods, a lobbyist for Northrop Grumman, was at the fund-raiser for only a short period, but he had no problem setting up a meeting with Bentsen for a few days down the road. O'Lenick, who coordinates the Congressman's schedule, told me that United Broadcasting could do the same. I was introduced to another staffer, Vince Willmore, who asked, "What are United Broadcasting's concerns?" This caused me to fumble a bit as I had no idea of what my fictitious firm's concerns might be. After a few moments I said that others in the company would soon be contacting Bentsen's office about those matters, to which Willmore replied, "Just drop on by."

Having established the groundwork for future contacts, I decided to call it a night. Departing along with me were two lobbyists for energy companies. As we reached the street one sighed, "Now to La Brasserie." That is the name of another popular beltway eatery favored by power brokers and politicians, and the site that night for a fund-raiser for energy industry poster boy Rep. Dan Schaefer of Colorado, hosted by a consortium of natural gas companies.

When Corporations Rule the World

That lobbyists play a central role in the nation's political life, as I witnessed during my brief career as a beltway hot shot, is not in itself surprising. In fact, lobbying is a practice almost as old as the republic. By 1852, as Jeffrey Birnbaum noted in his book *The Lobbyists*, future president James Buchanan was already complaining in a letter to another future president, Franklin Pierce, about the "host of contractors, speculators, stock jobbers and lobby members which haunt the halls of Congress."

During the past quarter century, though, the lobbying industry has exploded. Today, the "H" to "K" street corridor in downtown Washington is infested with law offices, consulting firms, public relations companies, polling agencies and lobby shops that effectively form the fourth branch of government.

There are an estimated 40,000 to 80,000 lobbyists at work in Washington—roughly 75 for every member of Congress even if one accepts the low end figure.

This huge army of influence peddlers, the great majority whom work for business interests, have greatly enhanced Corporate America's force in the capital. One statistic speaks volumes: In 1995, Congress showered businesses with $167 billion in "fiscal incentives," "export-promotion support" and other subsidies—in plain English, corporate welfare—a figure that dwarfs the $75 billion that was allocated during the same year to pay for all social welfare programs.

The rapid growth of the lobbying industry has occurred because business—spurred into action by the populist upsurges of the 1960s and 1970s, especially anti-corporate campaigns led by Ralph Nader and the more general upheavals surrounding the Vietnam War and the Watergate scandal—has become far more aggressive in seeking to influence government policy. In the early 1970s, most big companies didn't even maintain Washington offices. Today, some 600 corporations operate in the capital, as do an estimated 5,000 national trade and business membership groups. Most of these companies and organizations run in-house lobby shops, while depending on hired guns from outside firms to provide supplemental firepower.

During this same period, the world of lobbying has been transformed at the strategic level of tactics as well. Until as recently as a decade ago, lobbyists unbuckled vast sums of money to directly subsidize the day-to-day life of elected officials. The former head of Grumman's Washington offices, Gordon Ochenrider, filed a disclosure form in 1986 that revealed $12,093 worth of meals, liquor, flowers, entertainment at the Kennedy center, fees at the Washington Golf and Country Club, and tickets to sporting events. "Christmas used to be a wild time," recalls Jake Lewis, a long-time staffer to two legendary Texas populists, Reps. Wright Patman and Henry

Gonzalez. "Lobbyists would drop by the offices with buckets of booze, cigarettes and other goodies. They'd pass out plenty of stuff unless you turned them down, and there were few who did."

Sponsoring junkets, especially to exotic overseas locations, was another way for lobbyists to curry favor with lawmakers. In 1990, ABC's *Prime Time Live* caught a group of nine House members, along with family members and aides, at a resort in Barbados. Transportation to the island and hotel bills had been picked up by taxpayers while corporate lobbyists who had accompanies the junketeers helped cover daily expenses. In one scene filmed by *Prime Time*, lobbyist and former congressman Dawson Mathis puffed on a cigar as he pulled a wad of bills out of his pocket to pay for jet-ski rides for two merry members of the trip. Robert Macari, who became a lobbyist after serving as chief of staff to Rep. Marty Russo of Illinois, hosted a dinner and calypso concert for the entire congressional delegation on Barbados.

Other lobbyists relied on less orthodox if more direct means to win Congressional support for their clients. In Ronald Kessler's book *Inside Congress*, long-time senate staffer Roy Elson recalls that for many years lobbyists routinely supplied women to elected officials. "There was a cathouse right across from the New Senate Office Building where the Hart building is," Elson was quoted as saying. "They were mainly housewives who were making a little extra money. Some members went across to it [courtesy of lobbyists]."

The straightforward cash bribe was long an accepted practice as well. J.D. Williams, a former aide to Oklahoma Senator Robert Kerr and later the founder of Williams & Jensen, explained to *Legal Times*:

"Back in the old days, it was a common occurrence that [lobbyists] walked around with envelopes of cash in their pocket. One time I had mistakenly given a fairly junior member of a committee the envelope for the chairman of the committee. I sensed this when I received a call from the [junior] committee member saying how nice it was, what I'd done, and that 'I knew we were friends, but I didn't know we were that good.'

"For the most part, the bucks were passed in private. Only rarely did anyone get a glimpse of just how much money was rolling in. There was a high-ranking member of Ways and Means, a crusty old guy from the South who'd been there...forever. Everyone in Longworth [House Office Building] had a little brown safe in the wall. And when he died, they opened this guy's safe. And they took shoe box after shoe box of $100 bills out of that safe."

This truly was a golden age of lobbying. As *Campaign & Elections* magazine once wrote of the period, "There was a time when lobbying was strictly a backroom affair. Affable men in suits would hang around swarming, sweaty legislative chambers, buttonholing lawmakers as they swaggered through lustrous bronzed doors, whispering in ears, slapping backs, winking knowingly. These were the same men who were always good for a free lunch, a round of cocktails, and at election time, a check from their fainthearted clients."

Though this backroom world is far from extinct, lobbyists have been forced to develop new tactics as legal restrictions and tighter disclosure rules dampened the effectiveness of time-honored techniques. Cash bribes passed under the table were replaced by campaign checks passed across the table. In a similar transition, junkets have given way to "fact-finding missions," where lawmakers give a speech or appear on a panel in exchange for room and board at some cushy resort (though lobbyists are barred from paying for frills such as Jet Skis or golfing fees).

Producing a more profound change in strategies has been a growing public cynicism about business power, which has led corporations to disguise their direct involvement in lobbying campaigns. The most direct consequence has been an explo-sion of fake "grass-roots" mobilizations. Back in 1993, Burson-Marsteller was hired by the oil industry to help build opposi-tion to an energy tax proposed by Clinton. A company execu-tive, Jim McAvoy, was charged with coordinating rallies in small towns across the country. Just a decade earlier, the energy industry could have killed the tax with a handful of beltway lobbyists, McAvoy lamented to the press at the time. "Now you have to hire 45 people and send them to 23 states because all the noise is supposed to have more credibility."

In addition to "grassroots" activities, corporations now com-plement traditional lobbying with a multitude of other tricks: paying think tanks and "third party" experts to do their intel-lectual dirty work and testify on their behalf at public hearings and academic conferences; forming "independent" front groups to lead business-backed campaigns; hiring public relations firms to spin their message and manipulate the media. "In the modern world, few major issues are merely lobbied anymore. Most of them are now managed, using a triad of public rela-tions, grassroots mobilization, and lobbyists."

Congress: Training Grounds for Real Jobs

While pundits complain of a lack of civility between the two big political parties, the world of lobbying is politely bipar-tisan. That's probably because much of the supposed ideologi-cal difference between Democrats and Republicans is nothing more than partisan posturing. Scratch beneath the surface and it's clear that the two parties stand for virtually the same thing, namely, corporate rule.

Lobbying powerhouse Powell-Tate is headed by Jody Powell, ex-spokesman to President Jimmy Carter, and Sheila Tate, for-mer spokeswoman to President Ronald Reagan. Rep. Bob Walker, who while in Congress was one of President Clinton's leading critics, retired in 1996 and immediately took a job at the Wexler Group, a firm headed by Betsey Wright. Wright is a former aide to Clinton whose prime mission during her many years of service was to quell the "bimbo eruptions" that periodically surfaced in connection to the boss's extracurricular romantic entanglements.

Just as illuminating of Washington's bipartisan nature is the case of Bob Dole. During the 1996 presidential campaign, he told voters he would "go home" if he was defeated in his bid for the presidency. Most people thought Dole was referring to Russell, Kansas, but it turned out that the senator—who did after all serve for more than three decades in the capital and resided for a great deal of that time at the Watergate Hotel— had Washington in mind. After his defeat, Dole took up residence at Verner, Liipfert, Bernhard, McPherson and Hand, one of the most staunchly Democratic firms in the beltway. His colleagues there include George Mitchell, the one-time Democratic senate majority leader, and Lloyd Bentsen, the former Texas senator and treasury secretary under Bill Clinton. Dole's first act, though, was true to his G.O.P past: he offered a $300,000 loan to Newt Gingrich, which allowed the House Speaker to pay a fine imposed by the Ethics Committee over Gingrich's shady fund-raising methods.

For lawmakers and retired government leaders, lobbying is an alluring field because it holds out the prospect of easy money. Bob Packwood, the Oregon senator who stepped down as chairman of the Senate Finance Committee in 1996 due to allegations of sexual harassment made by female staffers, colleagues and reporters, confided to his fatal diaries that he regarded the U.S. Senate where he dwelled for 27 years as but a stepping stone to a more lucrative career as an influence peddler. Perhaps someday, he mused, "I can become a lobbyist at five or six or four hundred thousand" dollars a year. Indeed, less than a year after he resigned in disgrace, Packwood formed a firm called Sunrise Research and was representing timber firms and other corporate clients seeking lower business taxes.

Robert Packwood: The former Oregon senator pushed through the revolving door with the ambition of "becom[ing] a lobbyist at five or six or four hundred thousand" dollars per year. Packwood's resignation from the Senate in the wake of sexual harassment allegations did not deter him from setting up shop as Sunrise Research, a corporate lobbying firm.

Packwood's trip through the revolving door is a common one. Read the *National Journal* or *The Washington Post*'s "Inside the Loop" column and you'll learn of a regular stream of former members of congress and their staffers who go on to lobby for big business. According to the *Wall Street Journal*, forty percent of the members of Congress who were defeated in their election bids in 1992 later joined major law firms that do lobbying and consulting. Between 1988 and 1993, 42 percent of all permanent Senate committee staff directors became lobbyists, while the corresponding number on the House side was 34 percent. A senate staffer turned lobbyist told Jeffrey Birnbaum that working for the government was a bit like serving an internship for a doctor, saying ,"It's a card you have to punch."

As the Packwood story indicates, dishonorable years in the U.S. capital are no obstacle to a profitable career as a lobbyist. The *Washingtonian* writes, "In the lobbying world, developing a reputation as something of a rascal isn't necessarily negative— if you can deliver the bridge, or the vice president, to your client. What matters on this turf is winning."

Indeed, lobby shops view former members of Congress, scandal-tainted or not, as prized acquisitions since they are superbly suited to aid the corporations that they were supposed to be overseeing while in Washington. Consider Minnesota Senator Dave Durenberger, who specialized in health care issues during his 16 years in the upper chamber and retired in 1994 under a cloud of scandal. Durenberger took a job at APCO Associates, where his clients included Allina Health System, St. Jude Medical and several other health care interests. Susan Bartlett Foote, who served as Durenberger's senior legislative assistant and who wed him in 1995, worked with the retired senator in shilling for the health care industry.

Dennis DeConcini, a member of the S&L scandal's Keating Five gang, chaired a Senate committee that oversaw drug patents until retiring in 1995. He swiftly moved to Parry and Romani Associates, a firm run by his former chief of staff, Romano Romani. At his new home, DeConcini represents pharmaceutical makers like Pfizer, Genetech, Pharmacia & Upjohn, and Glaxo-Wellcome, the world's largest drug company.

The latter firm hired Parry and Romani to maintain a loophole in the GATT treaty that extends patents on drugs such as Glaxo's Zantac. That loophole, which remains unclosed with DeConcini's help, is worth millions to the drug maker because it prevents consumers from buying cheaper generic alternatives to Zantac until 1999.

Then there's Beryl Anthony, whom Arkansas voters ejected from Congress in 1992 after he bounced 109 checks at the House bank. After losing office, Anthony—who had served on the House Ways and Means Committee and is an old crony of Bill Clinton's—took a job with Winston & Strawn, where he specializes in regulatory issues. One of his first clients was the American Hospital Association, which told *National Journal* that Anthony was hired because of his "knowledge of the Clinton inner circle and his long friendship with Mr. Clinton."

Anthony's years of public duty were marked by a fervent devotion to pharmaceutical companies, which richly subsidized his runs for office. At Winston & Strawn, Anthony was hired by drug makers such as Pfizer and Bristol-Myers Squibb, who paid him to protect Section 936 of the IRS code, a corporate welfare program which gives American firms operating in Puerto Rico tax breaks worth billions annually. "That so many members of Congress—even ones who leave office in disgrace—become lobbyists and land in a financial bed of roses is very instructive to the colleagues they leave behind," says Bill Hogan of the Center for Public Integrity.

The revolving door pattern also holds true among former administration officials. A study from the Center for Public Integrity found that between 1974 and 1990, half of all senior officials who left the U.S. Trade Representative's office went to work as foreign lobbyists. In 1993, *Washingtonian* ranked the capital's most persuasive influence peddlers. The top ten included Stuart Eizenstadt, formerly Jimmy Carter's top domestic advisor; Tom Korologos and Bill Timmons of Timmons & Company, both who previously were employed in the Nixon White House; Patrick Griffin, a one-time Democratic aide in the senate who later became Bill Clinton's congressional lobbyist; and Lloyd Cutler, White House counsel to Jimmy Carter and later for Bill Clinton.

Thanks to its bottomless pockets, the tobacco industry has had great success in luring public officials to work on its behalf. At least five former high ranking lawyers from the Food and Drug Administration now offer their services to the tobacco barons. Richard Merrill, a former chief counsel at the FDA, now works for legal giant Covington & Burling where he represents all five cigarette companies as well as the Tobacco Institute. When asked about this apparent conflict Merrill told the *Wall Street Journal*, "I have absolutely no comment about that." Similarly mute about his labors for the tobacco makers is Richard Cooper, another former FDA chief counsel, who now works for R.J. Reynolds.

Access: Washington's Most Prized Commodity

In addition to their skill at rewriting the rules, retired government officials make for especially effective lobbyists because they have easy access to former colleagues. Ex-members of Congress are allowed on the House floor (though they are not supposed to lobby while there) and are permitted in private dining rooms and other restricted spots reserved for elected officials. A 1993 story in the *Wall Street Journal* found Ed Jenkins of Georgia, who in his post-House career has served as a lobbyist for companies like Lockheed, Pfizer, Delta and Hartford Insurance, was a regular at a weekly poker match with members of Congress. Guy Vander Jagt, a former Michigan representative who had moved on to Baker & Hostetler, was still invited to a regular Tuesday night dinner with House Republicans, as well as to the bipartisan weekly prayer breakfasts held at the Capitol. "If a lobbyist has worked on the Hill, he's going to get his phone calls returned," says Jake Lewis. "It certainly gives you a leg up on the competition."

For lobbyists who haven't served in Congress, gaining access to lawmakers is a vital priority. When lobbying for agricultural interests in the early-1980s, Paula Parkinson took a direct approach to achieving this goal. She claimed to have had sex with eight members of Congress, a relatively small number in the context of the full House but a voting bloc equivalent to the combined states of Vermont, Hawaii, Idaho and New Mexico. Parkinson took a 1980 golf trip with three members of Congress—Dan Quayle of Indiana, Tom Railsback of Illinois and Tom Evans of Delaware—all who subsequently voted Parkinson's way on a crop insurance bill.

Having a family member in Congress is also helpful, as seen in the case of Randy DeLay, the deadbeat brother of House Whip Tom DeLay. Until the early 1990s, Randy's financial prospects were grim indeed. Four business ventures in which he was involved—a restaurant, two oil projects and investments in beach property—had gone under. Shareholders in one of the oil ventures sued DeLay, in a dispute that was later settled out of court. In another case, DeLay's uncle and four other business partners sold a company called Oilfield Distribution out from under Randy and the new owners fired him from his $120,000 per year post as the firm's CEO. As a result of these setbacks, DeLay filed for bankruptcy in 1992.

Salvation came in early 1995, when Tom was elected to the whip's post. A number of big firms and trade associations promptly began to hire Randy as a lobbyist, though he had no previous experience. His clients have included Houston Lighting and Power; Cemex, the Mexican cement monopoly; Union Pacific Railroad and the city of Houston, which is home to both DeLays.

An article by Michael Berryhill in the *Houston Press* reports that between 1995 and mid-1997, Randy DeLay earned $750,000 in fees and expenses. The man who just five years earlier had been forced to seek refuge in bankruptcy now has a plush office in a Houston high-rise and regularly flies to Washington to meet with clients.

Of course, Randy's clients hire him purely because of the vast talents he displayed as a businessman, not because of his blood ties to the third most powerful Republican in the House. Tom, for his part, promises that he offers his brother no special favors. "Be assured there is no conflict of interest," he wrote in a statement issued earlier this year. "I have taken steps to make Randy's access to my office more difficult than any other registered lobbyist." Given the manner in which Tom has turned his office over to lobbyists, this statement, even if true, is hardly reassuring.

Where Does Microsoft Want to Take Us Today?

Software giant Microsoft's lobbying programs are directed by a large army of former members of congress and government officials. Of the six dozen people who registered to lobby for the company between 1996 and 1997, at least 57 have government experience. Four are retired members of Congress and 44 are former Capitol Hill staffers. Eighteen of the latter group worked for current members of Congress; at least six company lobbyists worked for the Judiciary Committee, which oversees policy on antitrust, immigration and intellectual property, three of the most important issues to Microsoft. Four company lobbyists have executive branch experience. Two are conservative activists with links to the highest tiers of the Republican Party.

Curiously, Microsoft didn't open a Washington office until 1995. When it needed help on the lobbying front, it turned to the D.C. office of Preston, Gates, Ellis & Rouvelas Meeds, whose partners include William Gates II, Bill Gates' father.

It was Microsoft's run-ins with the Justice Department over antitrust law that initially led the company to step up its beltway lobbying. And as Microsoft has grown, so has its Washington agenda. The company now lobbies on everything from porn on the Internet and software piracy to trade with China and tax policy. As a result, Microsoft's lobbying efforts have been rapidly expanding. Total expenditures in 1996 came to $1.2 million and the company unbuckled another $600,000 during the first half of 1997. In addition to its own in-house lobby shop, Microsoft retains 11 outside lobbying firms.

The company's hired guns have connections across the capitol, with Democrats as well as Republicans, from Congress to the White House. "Money is no object for Microsoft," says Bill Hogan of the Center for Public Integrity. "It's a company with a lot at stake in Washington so it hires [as lobbyists] who it wants, with the connections it wants, with the expertise it wants, and that means getting people as they come through the revolving door."

Probably no one is more important to Microsoft's lobbying efforts than Grover Norquist, who was hired in 1996 and is paid $10,000 per month. Norquist is one of the best-connected conservatives in Washington and is especially tight with Newt Gingrich. As one conservative activist says, "Grover is the easiest line into the Speaker's office. It's the most cost-effective way for Microsoft to do business."

Microsoft's connections to Gingrich don't end with Norquist. Also lobbying for the company is Vin Weber, a former House member from Minnesota who was one of the House Speaker's closest allies in Congress until he retired a few years ago, and Ed Kutler, who served as Gingrich's top policy adviser before departing in August of 1997.

The company's lobbyists have open lines with the rest of the GOP leadership as well. Dennis Stephens from Preston, Gates is a former aide to Majority Leader Dick Armey, while William Jarrell, also of Preston, Gates, formerly served as deputy chief of staff to House Whip Tom DeLay.

Microsoft is just as well connected to the Democrats. A key player here is retired New York Representative Thomas Downey, whose other lobbying clients include DuPont, Merck, Time Warner and Metropolitan Life. As a former member of Congress, Downey is always assured a warm reception on

Capitol Hill. He further greases the skids with old colleagues by making hefty campaign contributions—$26,250 during the last election cycle. Thanks to Downey's long-time friendship with Al Gore—he played Jack Kemp in the 1996 Veep practice debate—Downey has an open door at the White House as well.

Another high-profile Democratic lobbyist retained by Microsoft is Michael Lewan, who worked for 14 years on Capitol Hill, first for retired Rep. Stephen Solarz and then for Sen. Joe Lieberman. Lewan is also well connected at the White House. He was a trustee of the Clinton-Gore National Finance Council and is a managing trustee of the Democratic National Committee. "Lewan has access all over the Hill," says a lobbyist who knows him. "Staffers are below his radar screen; he deals with the members directly."

Former government officials were especially helpful in 1997 in winning approval in 1997 of the Software Export Equity Act (SEEA), which rewarded software exporters with a tax break worth $1.7 billion over the next ten years. The number one beneficiary was Microsoft, which hardly needs the help: the company's profits increased by 51 percent in 1996 to more than $2 billion.

The SEEA allows companies to exempt 15 percent of foreign sales from corporate income taxes. Microsoft and congressional supporters of the SEEA said the act merely gives software companies a tax deduction afforded many other manufacturers. Asked to comment about that argument, Robert McIntyre, head of Citizens for Tax Justice, replied, "Great, other companies get a stupid tax break so let's give it to Microsoft, too." Since it benefited less than 100 companies, the SEEA was automatically subject to a line-item veto by the president. President Clinton, however, failed to strike it from the 1998 budget.

The SEEA was introduced in the House by Rep. Jennifer

Dunn of Washington state, one of Microsoft's closest allies in Congress (she once publicly declared that company lobbyists are "on the inside group of advisers that I turn to when I need to discuss regulation issues and so forth"). Both of Washington's senators—Democrat Patty Murray and Republican Slade Gorton, whose former press secretary, Deborah Bruston, now coordinates Microsoft's state lobbying efforts—served as co-sponsors in the upper chamber.

Rob Nichols, Dunn's spokesman, said in an interview that his office has a "strong relationship" with Microsoft. According to Nichols, the company played a "pivotal role" in lobbying for the SEEA by "building grass-roots support" among Microsoft employees and Washington state residents.

Microsoft helped build support in Washington, D.C., too. The company lined up more than a dozen lobbyists to mobilize congressional and executive branch backing, including Norquist, Downey, Bruce Heiman, a former staffer for Sen. Daniel Patrick Moynihan, the ranking Democrat on the Senate Finance Committee, and Pamela Garvie, a former aide to Bob Packwood.

Microsoft and Oracle, another big software exporter that will reap vast rewards from the SEEA's passage, joined forces to hire a separate team of six lobbyists to lobby for the tax break. One of their joint hires was Kathleen Kies of Collier, Shannon, Rill & Scott, whose other clients include UPS, Total Petroleum, Inc., and the National Association of Convenience Store Owners. Kies is married to Kenneth Kies, staff director of the Congressional Joint Committee on Taxation and one of the most powerful staffers on Capitol Hill. According to *Fortune*, Kenneth Kies is "the man to see when it comes to altering the nation's tax code," adding that he had "ghosted virtually every line" of the massive 1997 tax bill which included Microsoft's tax break.

Microsoft and Oracle also helped put together the

American Alliance for Software Exports (AASE), which Nichols described as one of the most active Beltway proponents of the Software Export Equity Act. Its role was to drum up support for the tax break by mobilizing state and regional software associations.

Neither Microsoft or Oracle is listed on the AASE's membership roster, which boasts names such as the Information Industry Association and the Ben Franklin Technology Center of Southeastern Pennsylvania. But industry and congressional sources confirmed that the two firms were leading players in the alliance.

The AASE, now defunct, was a mysterious group. Its executive director, a political consultant named Doug Larkin, refused during a phone interview to disclose the group's budget or funders. When I stopped by the downtown Washington address listed on the group's letterhead, I discovered that this supposed grass-roots outfit had operated out of Oracle's downtown lobby shop.

Incidentally, Larkin now heads the Alliance for a Secure Tomorrow, a group which sounds like it was formed to oppose nuclear war or international terrorism, but which actually will act to generate support for Microsoft's position on the sale of encrypted software.

Access in Action: The Case of Robert Strauss

Friends, social partners, political confederates. All of this makes for a very cozy relationship between lobbyists and elected officials and allows lobbyists to win favors for their high-paying clients. This is clearly illustrated in the case of Robert Strauss, the legendary fixer and name partner at Akin, Gump, Strauss, Hauer & Feld.

Strauss has worked in Washington for decades and is as fixed in his eminence as any Supreme Court Justice. He served as chairman of the Democratic National Committee, re-election campaign chairman for Jimmy Carter and a special trade representative under the Georgia peanut farmer. In the spirit of bipartisanship, Strauss also worked for Republican administrations, serving on a presidential commission on Central America formed by Ronald Reagan, and as U.S. ambassador to Russia, a post he was appointed to by George Bush and which he held between 1991 and late 1992.

After returning from Russia, Strauss rejoined the Washington office of Akin, Gump, where he had toiled for many years before departing for Moscow. A tune sung by revelers at Strauss's birthday a few years back illustrates the law firm's smug self-assurance: "We keep all well-heeled oil men out of trouble, protect each cattle baron's precious rump, recession times we only charge you double, at Akin, Gump."

The prestige of the country's 19th-largest law firm, Akin, Gump, soared to new heights during the early Clinton years. Among its dozens of clients, many who signed up after Clinton took office, have been AT&T, American Airlines, Pharmacia & Upjohn, Loral Corp., Westinghouse, Warner-Lambert, Bechtel, Pfizer, Bank of America and several major insurance firms and associations.

Working alongside Strauss are Joel Jankowsky, known as the "Wizard of Oz" on Capitol Hill because of his behind-the-curtain role in many deals, and Donald Alexander, a former Internal Revenue Service Commissioner and the firm's tax specialist.

Also at the firm is Vernon Jordan, who, even more than Strauss, is Akin, Gump's chief rainmaker. A 1993 article in *Business and Society Review* found that Jordan sat on the board of ten major firms—American Express, Bankers Trust New York, Corning, Dow Jones, J.C. Penney, RJR Nabisco, Ryder Systems, Sara Lee, Union Carbide and Xerox—of which eight retained his law firm. Jordan is a friend of Bill Clinton's and took a leave of absence to serve as chairman of the Clinton-

©1991 Shia photo/Impact Visuals

Robert Strauss: His firm of Akin, Gump works to promote trade with China and other dictatorial regimes, as well as calling for increased harpooning of the world's endangered whales. When not busy raping-and-pillaging for Corporate America, Strauss works in government, for both Democratic and Republican administrations.

Gore transition team. He is said to have selected a number of top cabinet and sub-cabinet administration appointees.

Strauss also recommended many names, including that of Robert Rubin, first head of the National Economic Council and later of the Treasury Department. Strauss in 1991 rented out the "F Street Club" and hosted a party to introduce Rubin—then a superstar on Wall Street due to his exploits as vice chair of Goldman, Sachs, but mostly unknown in the capital—to Washington's elite. Attendees included the latePamela Harriman, Katherine Graham, Senator Bill Bradley and other leading capital socialites.

Five Akin, Gump lawyers took jobs in the Clinton administration while seven lawyers now with the firm formerly worked
in the federal government or for congress. Akin, Gump's influence in the capital is enhanced by its Political Action
Committee, one of the legal industry's most generous according to the Center for Responsive Politics. The firm, its employees and employees' spouses give hundreds of thousands of dollars to political candidates every year.

All that cash adds up to a lot of calling cards. In late 1993,
the *Wall Street Journal* ran a list of 80 business executives who
have lunched with the president during the early months of his
tenure. At least a dozen had close ties to the law firm, including clients such as John Bryan of Sara Lee, Gerald Levin of
Time Warner, and Dwayne Andreas, head of agribusiness giant
Archer-Daniels-Midland. (In October of 1993, Andreas flew
to Washington from Illinois to host Strauss's 75th birthday
party.)

When dark clouds loom on the horizon, Akin, Gump-
linked firms have received timely assistance from the Clinton
administration. John Bryson of the SECcorp, a firm client,
asked the administration for help in obtaining $150 million
from Mexico after it pulled out of an energy project in that
country. The Commerce Department was soon on the case and
Bryson's money was returned, with interest. American
Express—one of the corporations on whose board Jordan sits—
scored big in winning the federal government's credit card contract away from Diners Club.

The clearest example of Akin, Gump's influence came with
its role in promoting U.S. investment in and trade with Russia.
The key here was Strauss, who while serving as ambassador
established a close friendship with President Boris Yeltsin. To
expand ties to Moscow, Strauss set up the U.S.-Russia Business
Council (USRBC), whose 38-member board of directors is

stuffed with CEOs from clients of Akin, Gump and/or friends of Strauss's. In the fall of 1993, the Council used a $250,000 State Department grant to organize a four-day trade fair in Moscow, which Strauss attended. Further assistance for the Council came from the Commerce Department, which appropriated millions of dollars to set up "business centers" in Russia to help U.S. companies set up operations.

In early 1994, hundreds of million dollars worth of deals were announced during Commerce Secretary Ron Brown's trip to Russia with 28 U.S. business officials. Four of the participants were from firms that are Akin, Gump clients (Westinghouse, AT&T, Enron, Dresser Industries), two were from firms on Strauss's board at the USRBC (Litton Industries, General Electric) and two were from firms who Strauss has lobbied for in the past (Rockwell International, Bristol-Myers Squibb).

Such coincidences don't stop there. During the trip, the Overseas Private Investment Council (OPIC), which provides financing and project insurance to promote U.S. exports, announced a $125 million loan guarantee—then the largest in its history—to back a telecommunications project between U.S. West and Russia. OPIC is headed by Ruth Harkin, wife of Iowa Senator Tom Harkin and until recently a top corporate lawyer for ... Akin, Gump.

Another government agency actively promoting business with Moscow is the Export-Import Bank (Ex-Im), whose vice chairman under George Bush, Eugene Lawson, is president of the USRBC's board of directors. Between 1993 and 1995, Ex-Im's president was Kenneth Brody, is an old acquaintance of Strauss's from the days when he worked with Robert Rubin at Goldman, Sachs. Brody labeled Russia a priority for the Ex-Im and promised to "look under every rock" to find money for deals with the country.

In 1993, the Ex-Im negotiated an Oil and Gas Framework

Agreement which will finance Russia's purchase of $2 billion in U.S. oil, gas and petrochemical equipment. Since Moscow is a bad credit risk, a special arrangement was made whereby Russian companies serviced the debt with proceeds from oil and gas sales, which were deposited in an off-shore escrow account.

A chief beneficiary of the Framework accord was Dresser Industries, a Dallas-based oil equipment firm which does business with Akin, Gump. Company CEO John Murphy, an old buddy of Strauss's who sits on the board of the USRBC, was one of the lucky few chosen to make the Moscow trip. And incidentally, Murphy also served as a member of the Ex-Im's advisory committee.

Another participant on the trip was Westinghouse, an Akin, Gump client and board member of the USRBC which signed three deals with public utilities and government agencies while in Russia. "The agreements could give Westinghouse a leg up on its competitors in the region by linking its fortunes with the country's nuclear and electric power businesses," a report in *The Energy Daily* said at the time. "Despite its enormous troubles, [Moscow] could offer Westinghouse fabulous opportunities."

The GOP and Lobbyists: Up Close and Personal

The Clinton administration's shady relationships with campaign donors and lobbyists has served to obscure an obvious fact: Try as they might, and they have tried very hard, the Democrats have not been able to whore themselves to big business with the same degree of success as the Republicans. Dan Schaefer, chairman of the House Commerce Subcommittee on Energy and Power, succinctly summed up the GOP's cozy relationship with industry lobbyists in an interview with *Energy Daily*: "We go to industry and we ask industry, 'What is it we can do to make your job easier and to help you in this competitive world we have,' rather than writing legislation and having industry comment on what we write."

The GOP's takeover of Congress in 1994 resulted in lobby-ists gaining unprecedented access to the halls of power. Beltway influence peddlers fanned out across the capital where they helped draft bills with Republican leaders, offered point-ers to staffers and even coordinated strategy as legislation was debated on the floor of Congress. House Whip Tom DeLay of Texas worked with a team of lobbyists from "Project Relief"—a coalition of 350 corporations and industry groups—in drafting a bill to gut regulations affecting industry. A lobbyist for energy and petrochemical industries wrote the first draft of the legisla-tion, which called for a moratorium on any new federal regula-tions for 100 days. Other lobbyists from Project Relief found this too timid and wrote successive redrafts of the bill, length-ening the moratorium to 13 months and making it apply retroactively. According to *The Washington Post*, "Each new version sharpened and expanded the moratorium bill, often with the interests of clients in mind—one provision favoring California motor fleets, another protecting industrial con-sumers of natural gas, and a third keeping alive Union Carbide's hopes for altering a Labor Department requirement."

This model of cooperation extended to other legislative pro-jects. Corporate chieftains were thrilled when Rep. Cass Ballenger of North Carolina took charge of the House subcom-mittee which oversees the Occupational Safety and Health Agency. Ballenger's concern for working people is seen in how he ran his family's plastic bag manufacturing plant in the town of Hickory. As he once explained to *The Washington Post*, one piece of equipment called a scoring machine was especially troublesome. "The clutch on it was mechanical and the dang thing always slipped. You'd be wiping grease off it and the cloth would get caught in the gears and, thwack, it would just cut your fingers off." Ballenger's approach was to tell such unfortunate souls, "See what can happen? Put the guard back on and don't do that again. You'd learn not to do that any-more"

By late January of 1994, fifty corporate lobbyists—represent-ing the oil, chemical, steel and construction industries—had drawn up a list of 30 recommendations to gut OSHA and pre-sented it to Ballenger. As the *Post* reported, "There was little doubt among congressional insiders about who benefited from each section." A plank from chemical industries would have weakened requirements concerning the labeling of toxic sub-stances at the workplace; a steel industry proviso would drop a requirement to keep track of work-related illness that do not require medical treatment, such as hearing loss; a clause insert-ed at the behest of mining firms would have reduced the authority of the Mine Safety and Health Agency, which has helped dramatically reduce mine fatalities since being founded in 1968.

Business lobbyists were particularly active in seeking to scrap the nation's environmental laws. Before preparing a rewrite of the Clean Water Act, Republican committee leaders assembled an "advisory group" of industry representatives and state and local governments. That group set up several sub-committees composed of industry lobbyists, one which submit-ted a 68-page memorandum to GOP legislative leaders that detailed changes sought by business.

At the behest of Senator Slade Gorton of Washington, cor-porate lobbyists drafted a bill to dramatically weaken the Endangered Species Act. The Gorton staffer who received the draft—prepared by representatives of the timber, mining, ranching and utility industries—forwarded it to the senator with a note saying, "The bill takes some getting used to, how-ever I think that [they] did a tremendous job of adopting your ideas and putting them into the bill."

Money: The Mother's Milk of Politics

Political and social ties help bring lobbyists and lawmakers together but it is cash that serves as the primary bond between the two, particularly as the latter are highly dependent on campaign contributions from the former. During the 1994 election cycle, $97.5 million—about half of all PAC contributions—poured out of Washington. About 20 percent of that amount came from a single zip code, 20036, which runs through the "K" Street corridor. Washington also provided political candidates with $17.2 million in large individual donations, $2 million more than second place New York and almost twice the amount of third place Los Angeles.

A healthy chunk of the cash outflow from the capital comes directly from corporate lobbyists. During the 1996 election cycle, lawyers and lobbyists shelled out $9.4 million in soft money contributions alone, the fourth highest figure after contributions from securities and investment firms ($14.9 million), real estate companies ($10.3 million) and the insurance industry ($9.8 million). Lobbyists also serve on candidates' fundraising committees and press their friends and associates to donate money, in addition to playing the more banal role of primary habitué of campaign fund-raisers.

A refreshingly candid discussion of the role between public policy and lobbyist-provided cash can be found in the Packwood diaries. When the senator was seeking employment for his estranged wife Georgie—this in order to reduce his future alimony payments—he "hit up" lobbyists and businessmen who owed him favors. One target was Steven Saunders, a lobbyist for Mitsubishi Electric Corporation. "Consider it done," Saunders responded when Packwood asked if he could put Georgie on a $7,500 a year retainer. Just days later, Packwood attended a Finance Committee hearing and sharply questioned an American executive about Japanese patent practices. He asked virtually the same questions that lobbyist

Saunders had submitted to a Committee staffer.

Packwood next turned to Oregon businessman William Furman, who along with a colleague offered to set Georgie up in business as an antique dealer. Packwood was not surprised by the offer, writing in his diary that Furman was "eternally appreciative to me" as a result of a tax break that he had inserted in a 1986 bill. "[Furman] says that but for what I did for him in '86...he'd be out of business. Now he's prosperous beyond imagination."

Packwood also called upon Ron Crawford, a lobbyist for Shell Oil, General Motors and the American Iron and Steel Institute. Crawford and Packwood had a well established relationship: the former raised money for the latter and the latter did favors for the former's clients. As Packwood gratefully remarked to his diary in 1991, as he wrote of Crawford's financial support for his re-election campaign, "the advantage Ron brings me is that much of his income is dependent upon his relationship with me."

And so Crawford too readily agreed to help out when Packwood asked. "He'll put up $7,500 a year for Georgie," the senator reported to his diary. "That's three out of three."

Lobbyist as bagman is such an established role that those who challenge it risk suffering harsh consequences. In 1994, Rep. Dan Burton of Indiana pressed Mark Siegel, then a lobbyist for the government of Pakistan, for a $5,000 campaign contribution based on Burton's perennial support in Congress for Islamabad. When Siegel balked, Burton complained to the government of then Prime Minister Benazir Bhutto and told Siegel that he and his lobby shop's employees would no longer be welcomed in his office if he didn't come up with the cash.

Siegel's contract with Pakistan was for $450,000 and, by the morals of Washington, the lobbyist should have been wise enough to fork over a tiny part of this haul to Burton. Siegel, though, is notoriously stingy and became highly agitated after

Burton began pressing him for cash. A lobbyist familiar with what followed says that Siegel decided to call the congressman, hoping to at least negotiate a reduction in the tribute demanded. After getting Burton on the phone at his office, Siegel made a long speech explaining that he was a Democrat and as a matter of principle only gave money to Democratic Party politicians. Therefore, he would not be able to deliver the $5,000.

Burton was thoroughly unmoved by this plea. His response to Siegel before hanging up was succinct: "That's gonna cost you ten."

Siegel was being not only cheap but shortsighted, as help on the fund-raising front invariably pays high dividends. As Tommy Boggs once wrote in the *New York Times*, the efforts of lobbyists in raising money "help brings influence, connections, and returned phone calls." Former Senator Wyche Fowler, a Democrat from Georgia, made the same point in "Speaking Freely," a 1995 report from the Center for Responsive Politics: "[I would] usually get a list of about 30 lobbyists [and start] calling them, asking them to be on my committee and raise me $5,000 or $10,000 by a specified date. And then they would call and say, 'Wyche, I'd like to talk to you about the agriculture bill or banking bill coming up next week,' you say to yourself, 'Well, absolutely.' How can you not?"

How Lobbyists Open Doors:
The Key to the Lincoln Bedroom

Most big Washington honchos maintain a harem of favored lobbyists with whom they have an informal political favors-for-campaign cash relationship. A prime example is Vice President Al Gore, who depends for money on a large stable of former staffers, many of whom now toil on behalf of some of the Republic's largest corporations and trade associations.

When Gore's role in the Donorgate scandal first became

public—the Veep did everything from shake down Buddhist monks who had taken vows of poverty to using a credit card to make calls to potential donors from the White House—the press appeared to be in a state of shock. As Dan Balz of *The Washington Post* put it, Gore had "long been called the Boy Scout of the Clinton administration, a politician of such integrity and personal probity that even Clinton has complained about the vice president's glowing press."

Gore, of course, has never been a political Boy Scout, least of all when it comes to campaign finance. Between 1987 and 1992, he raised almost $2.5 million as a senator from Tennessee, according to the Center for Responsive Politics. Gore oversaw the telecommunications sector from his perch on the Senate Commerce Committee and raised nearly 10 percent of that $2.5 million from the communications barons.

Dan Dutko, head of The Dutko Group, a major beltway lobby shop that specializes in representing telecommunications companies, has played a leading role in filling Gore's coffers ever since the 1980s. According to one source, the two men devised an especially effective technique by which Senator Gore would arrange a conference call with a group of about five telecommunications company officials and industry lobbyists. Dutko would participate in these calls as Gore's designated plant. After the future Veep made his pitch for cash, Dutko, professing to be moved by Gore's passionate interest in the telecommunications field, would agree to pony up a huge campaign contribution. Not wanting to appear to be cheap, the other conference callers would reluctantly match Dutko's offer and Gore would walk away with a nice haul.

The flourishing of the Gore-Dutko relationship coincides with Dutko's meteoric rise within the ranks of Democratic Party bag men. Though fairly stingy about donating his own money—in the 1995-96 latest election cycle Dutko gave the Clinton/Gore campaign $1,000 and the Democratic National

Committee (DNC) a paltry $750—Dutko is keenly adept at extracting cash from others. In 1996, Dutko was named national finance vice chairman of the Clinton/Gore re-election campaign, as well as to the DNC's Financial Advisory Board, a group charged with prodding donors into doling out $350,000 or more. His colleagues on the board include Hollywood movie mogul Lew Wasserman and Steven Rattner, the *New York Times* reporter-turned-investment banker. Following Clinton's re-election, Dutko was put in charge of the Democrats' "Victory" fund, which will raise money for the 1998 off-year elections.

When not drumming up cash for Gore and the Democrats, Dutko tends to matters at his lobbying outfit. Its clients include telecommunications firms such as COMSAT, the Competitive Telecommunications Association, DSC Communications Corporation, National Cellular Resellers Association and the Satellite Broadcasting and Communications Association. The Dutko Group also represents the Alliance for GATT, Citgo Petroleum and the American Plastics Council.

Dutko is a staunch Democrat as is his company's vice president, Mark Irion, a former staffer to ex-Senator Alan Dixon of Illinois. But, like many Washington lobby shops, The Dutko Group has been careful to cover all the bases. Its top officers include Kevin Tally, former chief of staff and campaign director to William Goodling, who now chairs the House Committee on Education and the Work Force; Ronald Kaufman, a deputy assistant to the President under George Bush; and Gary Andres, another former Bush staffer and between 1994 and 1996 a member of the "Thursday Group," the group of GOP lobbyists who met regularly with the House Republican leadership to plot strategy on the Contract With America.

Thanks to his links to the Clinton administration, Dutko tends to be in the right place at the right time. He was one of

831 guests who stayed overnight at the Lincoln Bedroom during Clinton's first term and was invited to a June 1996 state dinner with Irish Prime Minister Mary Robinson. Dutko was also in the crowd at a May 1996 DNC fund-raiser held at Gore's mansion, an affair that raised several million dollars (and which Dutko described to the press as "a very tasteful and modest event").

Dutko attended at least two of the infamous White House coffee klatsches. Irion was also an invitee, attending a coffee hosted by Gore in November of 1995. That event was for members of the Democratic National Committee's Environmental Leadership Council, though the Dutko Group's interest in ecology does not appear to extend beyond its representation of a firm called Empire Sanitary Landfill, Inc.

Though considered to be one of the top influence peddlers in town, Dutko spends little time lobbying on the Hill or testifying before Congressional committees. Instead, he exploits his access to broker meetings between his clients and administration officials, opens doors at government agencies and otherwise serves as a high-level political fixer.

Take Dutko's work for DSC, a Texas-based phone switching and computer equipment manufacturer. Two years ago, DSC was battling with several foreign competitors to win a $36 million deal with Telmex, Mexico's state-run telecommunications company. The company faced serious obstacles to obtaining the contract, especially as one of its chief rivals, Alcatel of France, owns a five percent share of Telmex and was considered to have the inside track.

DSC asked Dutko for help and the lobbyist put the company in touch with officials at the Commerce Department. Soon, the late Commerce Secretary Ron Brown was on the job for DSC, writing and calling Telmex chieftain Jaime Chico Pardo to press the firm's case. In early June of 1995, DSC announced that it had won the contract; weeks later it sent a $25,000 donation to the Democrats. At Dutko's suggestion, DSC sent an additional $100,000 to the Democratic National Committee last year, a gesture which earned the firm's CEO, James Donald, a thank you call from Dutko's friend, Al Gore.

The Dutko Group's other clients have also done well during the Clinton/Gore years. One big winner was AT&T Wireless, the cellular phone division of its well known corporate parent. Shortly before Congress passed the Telecommunications Act of 1996, AT&T's lobbyists inserted a clause that freed the company to merge its cellular and long-distance operations, and to automatically assign AT&T as the long-distance carrier for its cellular phone customers. The Justice Department had ordered the company to do precisely the opposite when, in 1995, it allowed AT&T to buy McCaw Cellular Communications, Inc. AT&T Wireless paid The Dutko Group $260,000 for its efforts.

Molten Money

Dutko is just one of many Gore intimates who have profited handsomely from their relationship with the Veep. No one has cashed in on his ties to Gore with greater success than Peter Knight, who served as Gore's chief legislative aide in the House and Senate for a dozen years, in addition to running his failed 1988 presidential campaign and heading his 1992 vice presidential effort.

In his spare time, Knight since 1991 has been a name partner at a powerhouse D.C. lobbying firm called Wunder, Knight, Levine, Thelan & Forscey. Among the roster of companies represented by Knight's firm are tobacco giants RJR Nabisco and Philip Morris, asbestos-maker Manville, the American Forest and Paper Association, Shell Oil, Westinghouse, and McDonnell Douglas. Knight brought $2.9 million in billings to his firm in 1995 alone.

In 1996, Gore secured Knight's appointment as head of the Clinton re-election campaign, though his friend at the time had limited experience as a political fund-raiser. He proved to be a fast learner. In less than a year, Knight is credited with personally raising over $19 million for the party.

As has been detailed by journalist Jeffrey St. Clair, one way Knight scored such big bucks was by hitting up clients with matters pending before the executive branch. In the spring of 1996, just months after it had donated $100,000 to the DNC, Knight's client Lockheed Martin was picked for a big environmental cleanup deal. Another prominent company on Knight's Rolodex is the Fluor Corporation, one of the dominant players in the lucrative field of environmental clean-up. In 1995, Knight helped Fluor win a $5 billion contract from the Department of Energy to handle disposal of radioactive waste at the Hanford Nuclear Reservation in Richland, Washington. The contract was awarded by the undersecretary of energy, Thomas Grumbly, a former aide to Gore and a close friend of Knight's. Indeed, it was Knight, who in 1992 worked for the Clinton transition team, who picked Grumbly for his job at the Energy Department. Between 1995 and 1996, Fluor and its PAC funneled more than $200,000 to the Democrats, including a single donation of $100,000 to the DNC in May of 1996, just two months before the Hanford contract was signed.

The Gore-Knight-Grumbly triumvirate also scored big in a series of dealings with Molten Metal Technology Inc., a Massachusetts-based hazardous waste disposal firm that Knight represented in Washington. The story, as detailed by *The Washington Post*, began in the spring of 1994 when Knight successfully solicited a $50,000 donation from Molten's president, William M. Haney III, to help endow a chair in environmental studies at the University of Tennessee. The endowment was in honor of Gore's sister, Nancy Gore Hunger, who a decade earlier had died of cancer.

Haney soon received effusive thank-you notes from both Gore and Knight. The latter told Haney that the endowment was a "very personal priority for the vice president" and that his contribution would "never be forgotten." Indeed, within a few days of making the donation, the Department of Energy tacked an additional $9 million onto a $1.2 million research contract with Molten to develop hazardous waste technology. An internal Energy Department memo concerning the deal stated, "This is the contract T. Grumbly wants to add $9 million to."

Another win-win deal took place the following year as Knight began searching for money to fuel the Clinton-Gore re-election bid. In April, Knight—who was then receiving a salary of $7,000 a month and stock options from Haney's firm—arranged for Gore to visit Molten's plant in Fall River. The veep gushed about Molten's "ingenuity" and called the facility a "shining example" of American know-how. A few weeks later, Haney wrote to Knight to congratulate him for "orchestrating" the veep's visit, saying "You hardly seemed to break a sweat in bringing the Vice President to Fall River." In early June, Haney, at Knight's request, attended a Washington fundraiser for the Clinton-Gore campaign and pledged to drum up at least $50,000 for the Democratic ticket.

For Knight, mediating Molten's relationship with Gore and the Democrats offered direct benefits as well. Gore's visit to the company's plant sent Molten stock soaring, from $18 a share in April, the month of the veep's excursion to Fall River, to $37 in November. That month, Knight cashed in a chunk of the stock options he received as part of his lobbying fee and netted a pre-tax profit of more than $90,000. In May of 1996, one week after Knight suspended work at his lobbying practice to take full-time command of the Clinton-Gore re-election bid, Haney sent his 12-year-old son Zachary a gift of $20,000 in Molten stock.

Financial Warlords

Another long-time aide to the veep is Roy Neel, who replaced Knight as Gore's top Senate aide in 1989 and then became his chief of staff when Gore assumed the vice presidency. Early in the Administration, Gore made deregulation of the telecommunications industry a personal priority, including development of the "information superhighway."

In the midst of these discussions, Neel discreetly left the White House to become president of the United States Telephone Association, the $13 million-a-year trade group of the regional Bells and local telephone service companies. These firms stand to make billions from the Administration's plan to reshape the telecommunications industry, especially Gore's plans to privatize the Internet.

When the election rolled around in 1996, Neel was charged with marshaling support from the companies that had benefited so handsomely from Gore's efforts. This, quite naturally, proved to be a simple task. Federal Election Commission records show that the top five telephone companies alone contributed $1.2 million to the Democratic Party in 1996. It should come as no surprise to discover that Neel's telephone association is represented by Peter Knight's law firm.

Perhaps the most notorious of Gore's financial warlords is Nathan Landow, a Bethesda, Maryland developer. Landow raised millions for Jimmy Carter in 1976 and was considered to be a shoo-in to be named as ambassador to the Netherlands. Then reports surfaced about hotel and casino construction deals between Landow and members of the Meyer Lansky and Gambino crime syndicates. Landow withdrew his name from consideration and quietly disappeared from the political scene.

Landow re-emerged in 1988, when he became a major backer of Gore's failed presidential run. Since then he has helped raise millions to facilitate Gore's political career.

This fundraising bought significant rewards, including invitations to two White House coffee klatsches. But Landow clearly expected his financial aid to the Veep to pay financial dividends as well. As the 1996 presidential campaign was unfolding, Democratic fund-raisers enticed a $100,000 contribution out of the impoverished Cheyenne-Arapaho. tribe with promises that the Clinton administration would return to it mineral rich federal lands in Oklahoma.

After the election, DNC officials advised the tribe to contact Landow. According to tribal leaders, Gore's crony requested as payment a 10 percent cut from all oil and gas receipts generated on any recovered lands. Landow also implored the tribe to hire Knight's lobbying firm to represent their interests on the Hill, for a retainer of $100,000 and a fee of $10,000 per month. Cheyenne leaders claim that the developer threatened to use his clout to "make sure those lands are never given back" unless they agreed to his terms. The Cheyenne got nowhere in its efforts to recover its land but exposure of the case proved so embarrassing that the DNC returned the tribe's original $100,000 contribution.

Not even the campaign fundraising scandals of 1997 slowed the Gore machine's quest for political cash. Early in the year, as revelations about the Veep's role in the Donorgate affair began hitting front pages across the nation, lobbyist Knight sent out a fundraising letter in his role as chairman of the Vice President's Residence Foundation. Knight informed potential donors to the Foundation—which was raising money to restore the old Naval Observatory, where Gore and his family reside—that in exchange for $10,000 they would receive a print of a Jamie Wyeth painting of the Observatory and, more importantly still, an intimate dinner with Al and Tipper.

CHAPTER TWO

INVASION OF THE
MONEY SNATCHERS

How Lobbyists Fend Off
the Public Interest
to Protect the Corporate Interest

"I've worked on the Hill for 14 years, and I never saw an
issue that got decided on its merits. That's not bad or good,
that's just the way it is."

—Steve Horblitt, former congressional aide turned lobbyist.

During the latter half of 1993, the biggest priority on the
Fortune 500's political agenda was winning congressional
approval the North American Free Trade Agreement with
Mexico and Canada. It seemed a hopeless cause. President
Clinton supported NAFTA but polls showed that the public,
despite a business-backed PR effort, was skeptical of the trade
pact. The AFL-CIO and other union groups vowed to defeat
NAFTA, as did a coalition of environmental groups. A number of small business groups whose members had also been hurt
by low-wage foreign competition further swelled the opposition front. Confronted by such broad resistance, Congress
appeared all but certain to vote NAFTA down.

Suddenly, though, the political winds shifted. Without
explanation, Congressional resistance melted away and

NAFTA was handily approved by lawmakers. What happened? Behind the scenes, the business community, which views free trade deals such as a bridge to cheap labor abroad, had launched a fierce lobbying campaign to save NAFTA.

Business' principal lobbying organization, USA*NAFTA, spent millions of dollars to promote NAFTA by hiring up lobbyists to blitzkrieg the Hill. Lobbyists held weekly strategy sessions at the Washington offices of Allied Signal, while others were regularly briefed and prepped for action by administration officials such as Howard Paster and Mickey Kantor. The Mexican government spent additional millions to advance the trade pact, money that paid for the services of 44 Washington lobby and PR shops, and 33 former U.S. government officials.

The Clinton administration did its part as well, throwing open the treasury doors in order to bribe recalcitrant members of Congress. To win the vote of Rep. E. B. Johnson of Texas required a commitment to build two more C-17 military cargo planes ($1.4 billion); for Rep. Bill Sarpalius there was a promise to reverse Clinton's earlier recommendation to cut helium subsidies ($47 million); for a group of 12 members of Congress from Florida to Louisiana, there was a special protection for citrus, sugar and vegetable producers ($1.4 billion annually for the sugar deal alone). By one estimate, the cost to taxpayers of such deals could have been as high as $50 billion.

The Fortune 500's successful campaign for NAFTA typifies the way that business throws its weight around in Washington. It also shows that when corporations come calling, Washington lawmakers toss the opinion of their constituents—and the public interest—out the window.

Top Gun: How Boeing Dominates Democracy

That corporations exert strong influence on federal policy is no shocker. But the full scope of their political power would come as a surprise to most Americans. Consider Boeing, which after swallowing up McDonnell Douglas in 1997 emerged as a corporation with annual sales of nearly $50 billion. That makes it roughly the 75th largest economy in the world, with a gross national product slightly larger than Egypt's and Algeria's, and just less than that of Chile and New Zealand.

With the merger, Boeing became the only domestic manufacturer of commercial aircraft and it will control a two-thirds share of the international market. The rest is held by its only competitor, Airbus, the four-nation European consortium.

Just as daunting as Boeing's economic force is the company's political power, which is reflected by the heavy hitters who sit on its board of directors. Members include Robert Beck, a director of Texaco and Xerox; John Fery, retired chairman of Boise Cascade; John Bryson, CEO of Southern California Edison; George Weyerhaeuser, chairman of Weyerhaeuser; and Harold Haynes, the former head of Chevron. Another member, until he resigned in 1996 to become President Clinton's budget director, was Franklin Raines.

The full scope of Boeing's power is revealed by its army of roughly 70 lobbyists, who work to bend federal policy—including tax law, the budget, telecommunications, health care, land use, utilities, environmental policy, labor law and international trade—to the company's agenda. In 1996, Boeing spent more than $5 million for its Washington lobbying. The company's minions pressed its cause before virtually every important governmental institution, including both houses of Congress, the White House, the office of the U.S. Trade Representative, the Pentagon, the National Security Council, the National Economic Council, as well as the Departments of Commerce, Transportation, Agriculture and Treasury.

Boeing lobbyists devote considerable energy to the chore of jacking up the military budget, understandable given that the company gets $2 billion in annual contracts from the Pentagon. McDonnell Douglas gets far more that amount and the merger vaulted the new Boeing into the position of the nation's second largest weapons contractor. With $15.9 billion in sales in 1996, Lockheed Martin ranks first, with annual receipts from the Pentagon of about $21 billion. (That includes the sales of Northrup-Grumman, which Lockheed purchased in 1997). Pentagon planning documents obtained by the *Washington Post* show Boeing or Lockheed will be the prime contractor on 60 percent of major new weapons systems, which means that the firms will split between them an enormous pot of about $360 billion during the next decade. The only possible threat to this happy state of affairs would be if Congress decided to cut military spending and shift funding to social programs, a possibility Boeing's lobbyists will no doubt zealously guard against.

The merger with McDonnell Douglas will strengthen Boeing's ability to win money from the Pentagon, an ominous development for taxpayers. The company already has a large role in several monstrous raids on the public purse, most egregiously the Air Force's F-22 fighter, which Boeing and Lockheed are jointly developing at a cost of $1 billion per plane. That figure will likely rise as the Pentagon grimly announces almost every year that unforeseen developments require appropriation of several billion more dollars to cover the plane's R&D costs.

Quite aside from such extractions from the public purse, the Boeing-McDonnell Douglas merger may have serious long-term effects on the quality of Boeing's civil aviation products. For many years, McDonnell Douglas has been legendary in the aerospace business for the laxity of its cost and quality controls and for the degradation of its boondoggling corporate culture, linked to Pentagon procurement. Aware of the perils of this military procurement ethic, Boeing executives in the past tried to maintain a rigid divide between its civil and military operations, zealous to prevent the former from being entirely corrupted by the latter. In the bloated mega-corp such concerns will be even harder to sustain and Boeing could degenerate into inert fiefdoms ruled by the faked procurement budget, the rigged test and the featherbed ethic of cost-plus.

A number of Boeing lobbyists specialize in "tax mitigation" and "tax avoidance," areas in which the company's record of success is spectacular. In 1995, Boeing not only avoided paying any federal taxes but received a $33 million rebate from the U.S. treasury, making its effective tax rate minus nine percent. This feat was achieved by judicious use of the Foreign Sales Corporate Tax Credit and hefty deductions for R&D costs. The merger with McDonnell Douglas will mean more cash back for Boeing. Using the same tools, McDonnell received a 1995 tax credit of $334 million from the IRS.

Although Boeing deposits little of its profits into the federal treasury, its lobbyists work hard at extracting plenty in federal subsidies and other forms of corporate welfare. Taking advantage of a provision won by the defense industry in 1993, Boeing is expected to present the Pentagon—that is, taxpayers—with a $1 billion bill for "restructuring costs" related to the merger. That means plant closures, layoffs and fat payouts to retiring executives.

Boeing has been particularly adept at raiding the till of the U.S. Export-Import Bank, which offers below-market loans to countries purchasing U.S. goods and services. The bank has been so generous in greasing the company's foreign commercial agreements—more than $1 billion for deals with China alone—that some in Congress refer to the Ex-Im as "The Bank of Boeing."

Boeing is pushing to ease rules that allow the Ex-Im to finance only those deals which involve 15 percent or less foreign-made content. Since Boeing increasingly ships out work overseas (the 737 tail sections previously made by workers in Wichita, Kansas, are now manufactured by Chinese employees earning about $50 per month) the company has been lobbying to have the foreign-content figure raised to 50 percent. And since Boeing and McDonnell Douglas both hold seats on the bank's Foreign Content Policy Review Group, it seems a safe assumption that the Ex-Im will ultimately decide in their favor.

As befits a company of its size, Boeing has a very active foreign policy. It is the country's largest exporter, selling about 60 percent of its merchandise abroad, and thus has promoted GATT and other free trade initiatives. As the company's 10-K report to the Securities and Exchange Commission notes, "sales outside of the United States are influenced by U.S. government foreign policy, international relationships, and trade policies by governments worldwide."

More specifically, it has major interests in countries such as Russia, which it sees as a vast new market for commercial aircraft; Saudi Arabia, which has bought billions of dollars worth of Boeing's AWACs radar planes; and most of all China, where the company sold one in ten of its planes between 1993 and 1995 and controls a seventy percent market share. Boeing's 10-K report to the Securities and Exchange Commission says that if Washington-Beijing ties "deteriorate significantly," the company's ability to sell commercial aircraft to China "could become severely constrained." This point was put more succinctly by Boeing executive Lawrence Clarkson, who has said that if the company loses its commanding share of the Chinese market, "We're toast."

To help maintain fraternal relations between the two nations, Boeing retains Patton Boggs and six other beltway lobby shops. The company's Washington offices serves as headquarters for its so-called China Normalization Initiative. As part of this effort, Boeing and other big firms with interests in Beijing have retained pro-China academics to draft newspaper op-ed articles and speak at public events, and produced upbeat videos and brochures that laud China and urge an expansion of U.S. trade with Beijing. "When Boeing comes to Washington to describe what it needs abroad it will now be on much more powerful ground," Jeffrey Garten, a former Under Secretary of Commerce under Bill Clinton, has said of the merger with McDonnell Douglas. "Its desires for the direction of American foreign policy will become more influential than ever." (For a full description of Boeing's and Corporate America's efforts to improve ties with China, see Chapter 4.)

Together, Boeing and McDonnell Douglas employ almost 200,000 workers and have operations in nearly every state. To minimize the company's labor costs, Boeing has led state-level initiatives to hack away at workers compensation programs. Plans pushed by Boeing would cut the amount of payments to injured workers and diminish the quality and extent of the medical treatment they receive.

Boeing also spends freely to influence environmental policy, with company lobbyists seeking weaker regulations on clean air, especially in regard to ozone pollution from jet engines and smoke stack emissions from factories. Another area of concern is hazardous waste disposal policy. As of 1994, Boeing was responsible for the clean-up of 40 Superfund sites on the national priorities list, with a potential cost to the company of hundreds of millions of dollars. "Superfund reform," a current battle cry of Boeing and other big companies, means getting taxpayers to pick up a higher share of costs for clean-ups.

Lobbying for Anal Leakage:
It's a Dirty Job But Someone Has to Do It

Lobbyists don't only target Congress and the White House. They also seek to influence journalists, researchers, consumer activists and other seemingly apolitical players who affect political decisions made in Washington. The result is that corporate lobbying corrupts not only the political process, but science, intellectual life and the media as well.

Procter & Gamble's lushly funded campaign to obtain Food and Drug Administration (FDA) approval for the fat substitute called olestra provides a good example. P&G has invested more than $300 million to develop olestra and Drexel Burnham Lambert predicts that the fat substitute could generate $1.5 billion in annual sales, making it the biggest money maker in company history.

Thanks to olestra, the English language has been enhanced by the terms "anal leakage" and "fecal urgency." Those euphemisms are used by P&G to describe the severe diarrhea, cramps and other side effects suffered by some people who have consumed food containing olestra.

While the gastrointestinal consequences of olestra are well known, a number of more serious questions about the fat substitute's safety have been less widely discussed. Olestra depletes carotenoids, an important nutrient found in fruits and vegetables that is believed to reduce the risk of cancer, heart disease and other chronic ailments. Just weeks before the FDA gave preliminary approval for olestra, the Department of Health and Human services (which oversees the FDA) issued its *Dietary Guidelines for Americans* which suggested people eat more fruit and vegetables "because of [carotenoids'] potentially beneficial role in reducing the risk for cancer and certain other chronic diseases." Olestra also affects the absorption of the fat soluble vitamins A, D, E and K.

There are many independent experts who challenge olestra's safety. Dr. John Bertram of the Cancer Research Center of Hawaii says olestra would "constitute a public health time bomb." Dr. Herbert Needleman of the University of Pittsburgh School of Medicine says it would be "clear folly to introduce this product into the diet of children."

To ensure that such matters remain largely hidden from public view, P&G has conducted a vigorous lobbying and public relations offensive. The twin goals were to win final approval for olestra from the FDA—a decision is expected in 1998—and to convince the public of the fat substitute's healthful properties.

The company PR effort began in earnest in 1995, as the FDA was preparing its initial evaluation of the product. The first step was lining up support in Washington, this objective being achieved via the time-honored method of campaign donations. The strategy was especially effective in Ohio, where P&G is headquartered. In February of 1995, four members of the state's congressional delegation—Sens. John Glenn and Michael DeWines and Reps. John Boehner and Steve Chabot—wrote Donna Shalala of Health and Human Services, who oversees the FDA, to argue that olestra "can be safely consumed." The quartet stated that economic issues were, of course, secondary to public health, but felt compelled to point out that olestra's approval would mean $17.8 billion to Ohio over the next 13 years.

In March of 1995, P&G's political action committee rewarded Boehner with $500; a month later it disbursed $2,000 to Chabot. Glenn and DeWines weren't up for re-election at the time, but P&G had already given each $5,000, the maximum legal contribution, for their previous campaign bid.

Co-opting the Do-Good Crowd

Realizing that consumer groups might raise concerns about olestra, P&G determined to head off potential opposition from public interest activists. To handle this task, P&G retained lobbyist Carol Tucker Foreman. Foreman is one of those Washington lobbyists who loudly boasts about their commitment to consumer causes while quietly championing the corporate agenda. A former assistant secretary of agriculture in the Carter era and founder of the Safe Food Coalition, she's a familiar sight at Congressional hearings, lobbying for tougher standards on inspection of meat, poultry and fish products. She also sits on the boards of public interest groups, sitting cheek by jowl with some of the most notorious influence peddlers in the capital: at Public Interest with former Under Secretary of Agriculture Ellen Haas; at the Center for Public Policy with Hill and Knowlton's Anne Wexler; at the Food Research and Action Center with former Agriculture Secretary Mike Espy and David I. Greenberg of Philip Morris.

But Foreman also heads a public policy consulting firm, Foreman and Heidepriem, whose clients include Aetna Life and Casualty and Monsanto, the St. Louis-based chemical giant. Foreman is a heavy-hitter in Democratic Party fund-raising circles. Her brother, Jim Guy Tucker, was lieutenant governor of Arkansas, who graduated to the governor's mansion in Little Rock when Clinton went to Washington. Tucker stepped down after he was convicted in the Whitewater affair for inflating property estimates used to support loans to him from Madison Guaranty Savings and Loan.

One of the press releases issued by Foreman's Safe Food Coalition back in 1993 praised then-Agriculture Secretary Espy's untiring efforts to "overcome the combined effects of inertia, ineptitude and industry influence that permeate Food Safety and Inspection Service." In due course it turned out that inertia and industry influence were high on Espy's personal list of priorities as agriculture secretary, as symbolized in his friendly relations with Tyson's Chicken, the poultry behemoth of Arkansas.

Foreman uses her status as coordinator of the Safe Food Coalition to line up support from consumer activists. For P&G, she invited healthcare watchdogs to attend P&G-sponsored luncheons around the country, where well-known chefs whipped up meals cooked with olestra. At one of these affairs, held at chic Kinkead's restaurant in Washington, participants were treated to clams fried in olestra, a lentil salad with an olestra-based dressing, grilled swordfish topped with an olestra sauce and dessert of pear tart featuring a pastry made with olestra.

Dietitians and nutritionists were also on hand to promote the virtues of the product. But since olestra had still not been approved by the FDA, participants were required to sign a statement freeing P&G of liability in the event of any untoward reaction.

Science for Sale

P&G also heavily influenced the FDA's review process. All evidence presented to the agency came from the company's research trials, though these were hardly rigorous. P&G tested olestra on a highly controlled population, almost all healthy people between the ages of 18 and 44. Testing with children lasted no longer than one week, far too short a period from which to draw any solid conclusions.

The FDA panel that reviewed olestra appears to have been untroubled by such shortcomings. Then, too, nine of the 17 panelists who voted to approve the fat substitute have links to the chemical and food industries. These include Bruce Chassy of the University of Illinois, whose research has been funded by Nestle and Dean Foods; John Doull, of the University of Kansas Medical Center who has worked for Pillsbury, Best Foods and several pesticide manufacturers; and David Lineback, who has served as a consultant to several food companies, including P&G.

Henry Blackburn of the University of Minnesota School of Public Health, one of five panel members who voted against approval, told me that the limited duration of P&G's clinical testing made it impossible to assess the risks of long-term, low-dose exposure to olestra. "The FDA did not conduct a disinterested peer review," he says. "The FDA staff worked closely with P&G and acted as a proponent of the company's petition."

P&G is one of the biggest advertisers and buyers of research in the country, and has a good deal of practice in the area of distorting science. A few years ago the company, the largest manufacturer of disposable diapers, was sent into a panic because it was losing market share to cloth diapers. The primary cause was that the public was concerned about negative environmental consequences of disposables. Some state legislatures were even debating bans on disposables.

P&G's response was to pay researchers to produce a "public policy study" which showed that disposables were no worse for the environment—and perhaps even better—than cloth diapers (because of energy and detergent used to clean reusables). P&G even ditched the term "disposables" and replaced it with "single-use." Soon newspapers were heralding the P&G study—"People Claiming Cloth Diapers Are Clearly Superior May Be All Wet," ran one headline. Within a year, the threat to disposables had evaporated; P&G's sales boomed again.

In regard to olestra, P&G has put dozens of "white hats" from the scientific and medical communities on its payroll, though this relationship is generally not noted when these experts testify before governmental bodies or otherwise lobby for the fat substitute's approval. During the FDA hearings on olestra the company's hired guns took over an entire floor of the Holiday Inn in Alexandria, Virginia. Among those on the company payroll are former Secretary of Health and Human Services Louis Sullivan; Ronald Kleinman of Massachusetts General Hospital at Harvard, a food industry consultant who argues that wheat bread is no better than white bread; Dr. William Klish of Texas Children's Hospital, who has said that gastrointestinal problems caused by olestra "are essentially the same as those you'd expect when you switch to a high-fiber diet."

Elizabeth Whelan of the American Council on Science and Health is an ardent champion of olestra. In a syndicated column she wrote in 1996—"The new skinny on snack foods" ran the headline in *The Washington Times*—she called the FDA's decision to offer preliminary approval for olestra "both tasty and satisfying...Within months we will be able to buy a variety of delectable zero-fat snacks—a real life case of getting something for (almost) nothing." Whelan's byline did not note that her outfit receives handsome funding from P&G, to the tune of $12,500 in 1995 and $10,000 the following year.

Louis Sullivan, Secretary of Health and Human Services under George Bush, works as a consultant for P&G. He has been featured in advertisements and promotional materials for olestra, addressed press conferences and written letters to the editors. In one dispatch to *The New York Times*, Sullivan—identified only as "the president of the Morehouse School of Medicine"—said that "all Americans can feel confident in the safety of snacks made with olestra."

Other P&G consultants have appeared at public forums and scientific events. Two of the company's hired guns, Penny Kris-Etherton of Penn State and John Foreyt of the Baylor College of Medicine, were panelists at a conference on fat and sugar substitutes held in October of 1996. So, too, were P&G's own John Peters, as well as representatives from food industry giants such as Kraft Foods and Nabisco, both which might use olestra down the road.

The conference itself was co-sponsored by the International Life Science Institute (ILSI), which receives much of its funding from the private sector, including P&G. The company also sits on the Institute's boards of directors and helped pay for the conference, though George Hardy, ILSI's executive director, would not reveal the amount of the contribution. Conference proceedings were later published as a bound volume in the *Annals* of the New York Academy of Science. The *Annals* are distributed to more than 700 libraries and, according to the Academy, "are among the oldest and most frequently cited sources of scientific research." Hence, future researchers investigating fat substitutes such as olestra will draw on evidence presented at a conference influenced by P&G.

P&G argues that the fees it pays scientific consultants are modest and unlikely to influence scientific outcomes. "These are known academics and health researchers who have built reputations for sound science over their careers," says company spokeswoman Jacqui d'Eon. "They are not going to be bought." John Stauber, editor of *PR Watch*, a newsletter which covers the PR industry, disagrees. He says P&G hires people "who appear to have some distance from the company, but they are carefully selected and can be counted on to promote the official line. There's nothing objective or independent about them."

Marion Nestle of NYU's nutrition department turned down an offer of $1,000 from P&G, for which she was to fly to New Orleans, give a short speech and eat products made with olestra to demonstrate her confidence in its safety. "It's too crude or imprecise to say people are bought off," Nestle told a reporter from the *Boston Phoenix*. "But I just know if somebody is giving my department money, then I would think twice before saying something mean about that particular industry." Nestle is a rarity. Numerous academics accepted P&G's money and went to New Orleans.

In Columbus, Ohio, one of the four cities where olestra-laden snacks were being test-marketed in 1997, P&G's PR campaign was especially intense. The company retained at least six advertising and PR agencies at a cost of millions of dollars, including two heavy hitters from the Clinton-Gore campaign: Penn & Schoen, a polling firm, and The Communications Co., an ad agency owned by the Democratic consulting firm of Squier, Knapp & Ochs.

As part of the effort in Columbus, P&G sent a 10-minute video on olestra to local groups such as the PTA. Accompanying the video, which featured Sullivan expounding on olestra's virtues, was a "fact sheet" prepared by the American Dietetic Association. The fact sheet's wording was virtually identical to that of P&G's own hand-outs, a logical resemblance since P&G paid for the fact sheet and provides significant funding to the Dietetic Association.

P&G's campaign for olestra is unusual in its scope, but reflects industry's growing influence on scientific research. A few years ago, researchers at the University of California-Los Angeles sought out doctors to help conduct a study on drug advertising. To guard against bias, the researchers planned to exclude doctors who had received more than $300 in consulting fees or other payments from pharmaceutical companies during the previous two years. The rules were abandoned when it proved impossible to find sufficient doctors that met the criterion.

How to Buy a (Committee) Chair:
Arizona Public Service Co.'s Washington Shopping Guide

The simplest, cheapest and most effective way to win favors in Washington is simply to purchase a willing member of Congress. Such a strategy isn't always an option—two prerequisites are the availability of a member influential enough to push through a given bill and an issue sufficiently obscure so as not to attract significant media attention—but when it is, companies can win truly extraordinary pay-offs on small investments. A worthy example comes with Arizona Public Service Co.'s acquisition, for roughly $20,000, of Sen. Frank Murkowski of Alaska, chairman of the Energy and Natural Resources Committee.

Back on January 18, 1997, Murkowski took a break from the Washington winter and flew to sunny Tucson, Arizona to address a conference sponsored by the Edison Electric Institute (EEI). The cost of the journey—$4,945.65 for transportation, food and lodging—was picked up by the EEI, the trade group for the nation's privately-owned utility companies and an orga-

©Rick Reinhard/Impact Visuals

Sen. Frank Murkowski: GOP senator from Alaska, Murkowski is one of the best buys in the upper chamber. In exchange for a mere $14,500, Arizona Public Service prodded him into introducing a bill in Congress that was drawn up by the company's CEO.

nization whose members have a broad range of interests before Murkowski's committee.

That night, Murkowski was the guest of honor at a campaign fund-raiser held at the home of Richard Snell, head of the Pinnacle West Capital Corporation. Pinnacle West is a holding company that owns Arizona Public Service Co. (APS), an EEI member and the largest electric utility in the southwestern United States. The affair brought in $16,500 for Murkowski's 1998 re-election campaign, of which $10,500 came from people linked to Pinnacle West or APS (including a combined $1,500 from Snell and his wife, Alice). Nine days later, APS's political action committee ponied up another $3,500 for Murkowski's campaign.

On March 13, less than two months after having feted Murkowski at his Scottsdale estate, Pinnacle West's chieftain was invited to testify before the Energy and Natural Resources Committee. Snell spent the bulk of his time denouncing the fact that Congress allows publicly-owned utilities to issue tax-exempt bonds, while denying that right to private companies like his own APS. "Such financing has cost the federal government revenues and led to distortions of the market," Snell told the committee. "If allowed to continued unchecked, [tax-exempt financing] will seriously compromise free and open competition."

To correct this supposed injustice, Snell proposed that public utilities be barred from marketing tax-exempt bonds unless they agree to sell electricity to customers only in their current boundaries. With deregulation of the utility industry advancing rapidly, Snell's arcane proposal would seriously weaken the ability of public companies to compete with their far more powerful private cousins.

Following Snell's appearance, Murkowski began quietly drumming up support for Pinnacle West's position in Washington, pressing the case with colleagues in Congress and with Clinton administration officials. Then, with Congress winding down, Murkowski on November 8 introduced Senate Bill 1483, which put Snell's proposal in legislative language. "Public power should not obtain a competitive advantage in the open marketplace based on a federal subsidy that flows from the ability to issue tax-exempt debt," Murkowski said upon introducing the bill in the Senate Finance Committee, where he also serves.

Murkowski's sponsorship of SB 1483 is typical of the dutiful service he performs for private utility companies, who rank among his top financial patrons. Indeed, even before

Murkowski had introduced the bill, Robert Aiken, a Washington lobbyist for Pinnacle West, had sent a confidential memorandum to 12 private utility lobbyists lauding the Alaskan senator for his undying efforts on the industry's behalf. "Our friend Senator Frank Murkowski has put the issue of public power tax-exempt debt on the front burner," Aiken wrote in his memo. Aiken added that Murkowski "seems to be willing to take this issue on" for the industry in Congress, and urged his lobbyist cronies—eight whom represent companies that have already made campaign donations to Murkowski in 1997—to "do all we can to support him."

Murkowski's shilling for private utilities makes sense from a campaign finance point of view, but makes little sense for his constituents in Alaska. As of 1995, private utilities provided electricity for only 8.5 percent of Alaskan residents. The rest are served by electric cooperatives and public power.

Power Lobbying

Murkowski's exertions for the private utility industry must be seen against the backdrop of the ongoing deregulation of the $212 billion electric power industry. Bills calling for deregulation—which will mean that consumers will no longer be required to buy power from their hometown utilities but can choose an electric company the way they now choose a long-distance carrier—have been moving slowly at the federal level, but thirteen states have already adopted some form of retail competition.

The 120 private utilities mustered in the EEI dominate the market, providing about 76 percent of the nation's electricity. Their leading competitors are public utility systems, which hold only a 14 percent market share. The rest is controlled by electric cooperatives, which were set up to serve rural customers, and federal projects such as the Tennessee Valley Authority. Public and private companies have been fierce rivals since the electric industry was founded in the late 19th century, with the latter generally being favored in Washington, especially in recent years.

Thanks to his post as chairman of the Energy and Natural Resources Committee, Murkowski is a key player in the deregulation debate and has been avidly courted by electric companies. Of the $163,383 in campaign money he raised from PACs between January and October of 1996, the biggest single chunk—$31,583—came from utility interests. Murkowski's utility PAC funds came entirely from private companies. Pacific Gas & Electric was the biggest single contributor, offering up $5,618. In second place was Southern California Edison with 3,965, followed by APS ($3,500) and Florida Power & Light and Houston Industries ($2,000 each).

Murkowski raised an additional $27,600 in individual contributions during the first 10 months of 1996. Utility companies and their lobbyists provided most of that amount, with the lion's share coming from private firms. In addition to hefty endowments from officials of Pinnacle West and APS, Murkowski also took in $500 from John Ogden, head of SunCor Development, Pinnacle West's real estate subsidiary.

Private utility firms have also been generous in sponsoring junkets for Murkowski and his staffers. Between 1996 and 1997, Murkowski and his staffers went on at least 15 separate trips financed by private utility companies or their trade associations (versus only two financed by public power providers) at a total cost of more than $40,000.

Murkowski himself made two trips, both to EEI affairs in Arizona. The leading frequent flyer from the senator's office was Chief of Staff Gregg Renkes, who made eight trips. Three of those journeys were financed by the Edison Electric Institute, including a January 1997 trip to Phoenix where Renkes participated in a meeting of EEI chief executive officers. Renkes also flew to Phoenix courtesy of Pinnacle West; to Juno Beach, Florida, to visit with Florida Power & Light; and to England courtesy of the Nuclear Energy Institute.

Though not a congressional staffer, Murkowski's wife, Nancy, has also taken trips on the industry's tab. When her husband went on a taxpayer-financed 10-day fact-finding mission to Hong Kong, Taiwan and Japan in December of 1996, the Federation of Electric Power Companies of Japan, which works closely with EEI, courteously shelled out $7,223.32 so Nancy could tag along.

In return for their blandishments, Murkowski has sided with private utilities on every major issue regarding deregulation of the electric industry. Murkowski, for example, supports deregulation, but unlike its more extreme supporters is against a federal mandate that would force competition by a certain date, instead arguing that states should set their own timetables.

That position is shared by Murkowski's private utility financial supporters, who want to reduce their costs and debts, and otherwise position themselves before competition gets underway. Furthermore, the big utilities are powerful political players in their home states and are in a strong position to influence policy in local legislatures. As the *Arizona Republic* wrote in an article about energy deregulation, "In the world of electric competition, Arizona Public Service Co. can be portrayed as a moose: a big, powerful, lumbering critter that pretty much does what it wants."

Along with Sen. Al D'Amato of New York, Murkowski is also co-sponsor of a bill that would for the first time allow a private electric company to purchase a utility that is not geographically contiguous to its current area of service. The bill is opposed by public power companies, who say it would hurt consumers by paving the way for excessive concentration of the electricity market.

All but three of the 21 private utility interests that have made PAC contributions to Murkowski this year have substantial investments in nuclear power, and Murkowski has been one of that industry's most avid supporters in Congress. The utilities sank enormous sums of money into big nuclear plants, which turned out to be hugely expensive to operate. They now want to recover hundreds of billions of dollars worth of nuclear-related debts—so-called "stranded costs"—from rate payers, instead of passing the cost on to shareholders. Without such relief, say the utilities, they won't be able to compete with non-nuclear utilities after deregulation is implemented.

In 1996, the California assembly passed a law deregulating the state's electric industry while simultaneously providing $16 billion from rate payers to bail out the Diablo Canyon nuclear plant (run by Pacific Gas & Electric) and the San Onofre nuclear plant (owned mostly by Southern California Edison). The bill was drafted in part by David Takashima, who left his job as a lobbyist for Southern California Edison to join the staff of Steve Peace, the state senator leading the deregulation drive. Takashima subsequently departed from Peace's employ to take a lobbying job with Pacific Gas & Electric.

The Edison Electric Institute wants to use California as a model for a federal rescue of the nuclear industry. So does Murkowski. On September 9, 1997, he sent a ten-page memo to his colleagues on the Energy and Natural Resources Committee, which contained his recommendations for how to implement "electric power industry competition legislation." A good chunk of the memo was devoted to ways that Congress can "retain the nuclear power option," including repeal of a law that restricts foreign investment in the sector and doing away with a requirement that the Nuclear Regulatory Commission conduct an antitrust review of all nuclear licensing actions. As to the issue of recovering stranded costs, Murkowski's "proposed resolution" is a "non-bypassable 'wires' charge." Translation: the nuclear industry will be bailed out with a mandatory surcharge on electric bills, paid by consumers and collected by the federal government.

Murkowski's memo champions nuclear power as clean energy, saying the industry "accounts for 89% of all the (carbon dioxide) emissions avoided by U.S. electric utilities between 1973 and 1995." Murkowski's enthusiasm here for environmental protection is ironic since he has supported gutting the Clean Air Act and strongly opposes a proposal by the Clinton administration that would moderately reduce industrial emissions of carbon dioxide.

But nowhere is Murkowski's devotion to his campaign contributors more apparent than in his promotion of Richard Snell's proposal on tax-exempt financing. Private utilities concede that they charge far more than public companies. Pinnacle West lobbyist Aiken attached a study to his confidential memo that shows that in Arizona, Arizona Public Service's average retail rates are 21 percent higher than those charged by Salt River Project, a public competitor; Florida Power & Light charges 12 percent more than the Jacksonville Electric Authority; the Southern Company, which serves parts of Georgia, Alabama, Florida and Mississippi, charges 55 percent more than its public competitors.

According to private utilities, the differential is largely accounted for by public companies' ability to market tax-exempt bonds, which significantly reduces their cost of borrowing money. Furthermore, public utilities have non-profit status and therefore pay no income taxes.

What the private utilities discreetly fail to mention is that they enjoy a number of advantages not shared by public power. As corporate entities, private companies can take advantage of tax write-offs such as accelerated depreciation. Congress voted to phase out investment tax credits in 1986, but many big companies still benefit from that loophole. Private companies are also allowed to issue tax-exempt bonds for the express purpose of pollution control. According to its 1996 annual report, APS has $450 million worth of such bonds outstanding.

Many industry observers agree that on balance, public power and private power operate on a level playing field. In a 1996 interview with *Congressional Green Sheets*, Holly Propst, administrative assistant to Rep. Dan Schaefer of Colorado —a leading Congressional supporter of private utilities and of electric deregulation—said her boss "had us look at this whole subsidy issue, and the further you tease that out and start looking at the tax code, it becomes less clear who wins on subsidies. Especially because [private utilities] get a lot of tax benefits." Schaefer himself told the same publication, "In all our talks with all our utilities, they'd like to see that go away, the tax thing for public power, but they understand what Holly was saying, that there's a balance out there."

Public utilities argue that private electric companies have used the tax-exempt provision as an excuse to overcharge their customers. "Now that these utilities are facing the prospect of competition, they are seeking to raise public power's rates to their own high levels, and raise taxes on millions of public-power consumers," Robert Claussen, general manager of the Alabama Municipal Electric Agency, said in a recent interview with *Inside Energy*.

Ever since Snell first floated his proposal before Murkowski's committee, Pinnacle West has been furiously lobbying in Washington to revoke public power's right to issue tax-exempt bonds. While the issue carries great importance for all private utility companies, it is of special interest to Pinnacle West. The Arizona state legislature has already passed a bill that begins phasing in deregulation of the utility industry in 1999 and Pinnacle's subsidiary, APS, faces stiff competition in the form of the Salt River Project, one of the few public power companies of significant size.

Aiken, Pinnacle West's top Washington lobbyist, conveniently heads the Edison Electric Institute's internal committee on taxation issues, which he has used to advance the assault on public power. He is working closely with the chief lobbyists for two other utility powerhouses, Buzz Miller of the Southern Company, who has also worked for the Nuclear Energy Institute, and Mike Wilson of Florida Power & Light, a former Florida public service commissioner. Wilson's company is a member of the elite Republican Team 100, which comprises $100,000-and-up donors. Last February, Wilson and dozens of other lobbyists and corporate officials joined a host of GOP power brokers, including Murkowski and House Speaker Newt Gingrich, for a private retreat at the Breakers Hotel in Palm Beach, Florida.

Murkowski is clearly Pinnacle West's most important asset on Capitol Hill. During his testimony in March, Snell fretted that the Internal Revenue Service was already reviewing public utilities' right to issue tax-exempt bonds. He worried that the IRS might renew support for that right, saying it would be "unfortunate" if the agency took action because "it is Congress that should be making policy at this level."

Just over a month later, Murkowski sent a sharply worded letter to Treasury Secretary Robert Rubin, who oversees the IRS. "I am...concerned that the changes the IRS is considering may allow publicly-owned utilities to expand the use of tax-exempt bonds to compete against privately-owned utilities," Murkowski said. "This is not the purpose for which Congress authorized publicly-owned utilities to issue tax-exempt bonds." Echoing Snell's testimony, Murkowski closed by saying, "This is a matter for the Congress to decide, not the IRS."

Murkowski sent three letters on the same topic to Rubin during the next seven months. The last, dated October 20, reiterated his "request that Treasury withhold issuing any regulations in this area," and warned that "the government should do nothing that would enhance the competitiveness of one sector of the industry against another sector, especially if such a decision would cost federal revenue." (Needless to say,

Murkowski did not request that the IRS close costly loopholes available to private utility companies.) As of early 1998, the IRS has issued no regulations on the matter, despite repeatedly saying that it would do so well before 1997 was over.

Murkowski has also been leaning on fellow members of the Energy and Natural Resources Committee. In the September memo to committee members mentioned above, Murkowski said that after "extensive review" he had concluded that since "tax-exempt financing substantially lowers the cost of construction, it would be competitively unfair to allow those who have built facilities with tax-exempt financing to use those facilities to compete against others who do not have access to this special tax exemption." Therefore, public companies should be prevented from "selling power from those facilities outside of their existing service areas" after competition is implemented.

With his introduction of SB 1483 in November, Murkowski went further. Public utilities seeking to sell outside their historic boundaries would not only be barred from issuing tax-exempt bonds, but would be required to buy back all of their outstanding tax-exempt bonds before they could compete against private companies. (Public utilities currently have a combined $70 billion worth of tax-exempts on the market.)

Murkowski's bill states that if his legislation is passed, it will take effect retroactively to November 8, 1996, the date he introduced it. The bill's ultimate fate is still not certain but since buyers of tax-exempt bonds issued by public utilities can no longer be certain that they will receive the full interest, its mere introduction had a chilling effect on the market. Frank Shafroth of the National League of Cities charged that introducing the bill had allowed Murkowski, "without any...votes from other members of Congress, or the signature of the president, to dictate federal law."

Murkowski appears to have worked closely with lobbyists for

Pinnacle West, and other private utilities, in preparing the legislation. Aiken's memo to his lobbyists cronies states that the EEI had sought "to support Senator Murkowski's effort on this issue" by conducting research into current debt loads held by public power companies.

Space Is Limited—Call Now to Reserve Your Bribe

Murkowski's bill is so tilted in favor of private utilities that some industry observers wonder about his true motives for introducing the legislation. "The suspicion here is that the measure is not really designed to deal with the problem of the various subsidies that currently distort the generating market," the *Electricity Daily* speculated. "Most likely, it's really about raising [private utility] money for Murkowski's upcoming 1998 senatorial reelection campaign."

Murkowski could surely use the cash. Despite always spending far more than his opponents, he's never won election with more than 55 percent of the vote.

Meanwhile, Pinnacle West is trying to build broader support in Congress for Murkowski's measure. As 1998 dawned, Aiken was circulating a memo around Capitol Hill that invited selected congressional staffers to a retreat and seminar at the Wigwam, a plush resort near Phoenix managed by SunCor Development, Pinnacle West's real estate arm.

Rooms at the Wigwam range from $320 to $465 per night, and the resort offers nine tennis courts, three golf courses, two swimming pools, a health club, horseback riding and hot air balloon rides. "Sunshine, gentle breezes and sparkling water," says the resort's brochure. "All the simple pleasures that make for magic times. Venture into the desert atop a trusty steed. Find time for dozing in the sun. Here, the escape is yours for the making."

Lobbyists and Nuclear Visigoths

Big money corporate lobbyists don't always win their battles, but when they are defeated it's rarely because Congress or the White House rises to defend the public interest. More likely, the scheme being advanced was so loopy that even official Washington was too embarrassed to take up the cause. That's the case with a multi-billion dollar plot put together by a cabal of beltway con men who hoped to dump tons of nuclear waste on a Pacific island. Despite having been defeated, the would-be scheme is noteworthy in showing that well-connected capital honchos and aggressive lobbying can keep even the nuttiest projects in play.

Money and politics make for strange bedfellows but the nuke deal was put together by what must surely rank as one of the most bizarre beltway coalitions of all time: a volatile Englishman who sometimes poses as a rock star, a retired CIA official, a self-described flower-child-turned investment banker and a well-known Friend of Bill.

The corporate vehicle for the plan is U.S. Fuel and Security Inc. (USF&S), a Washington-based firm. The company's CEO is Daniel Murphy, a lobbyist who formerly served as deputy director of the CIA and chief of staff to George Bush when the latter was vice president. Murphy carried out a variety of murky activities while in government, once accompanying the notorious influence peddler Tongsun Park to meet with then President Manuel Noreiga of Panama. Intrigue attaches to Murphy's post-government career as well. In investigating the nuclear story, I was told by an informed source that a frantic caller from South Korea had recently rung up Murphy's firm and demanded to know the whereabouts of a submarine that the former CIA honcho had promised him.

Murphy's partners at USF&S include Alex Copson, who has pawned himself off to a variety of reporters and government officials as the former bass guitarist (and sometimes the drummer) for the Sixties rock group Iron Butterfly. Why Copson believes that a rock and roll pedigree would heighten his credibility in promoting the nuclear dump plan remains a mystery. Then there's a Wall Street investment banker named Thomas Kirch, an aging hippie who, Copson says, "brings the peace, love and flowers" to the project. The firm has recruited a number of heavy hitters to its cause. USF&S's counsel is retired Secretary of State James Baker. Former FBI director William Webster sits on the advisory board of International Fuel Containers, a corporate subsidiary that plans to build huge steel containers to store the nuclear waste. Mark Grobmyer, a Little Rock lawyer and golfing partner of President Clinton's, has vigorously lobbied the White House on the company's behalf.

USF&S has also lined up international support. MinAtom, the Russian nuclear energy ministry, has indicated that it will sign on as a co-sponsor of the deal. The German firm GNB, Europe's largest producer of fuel storage casks, has given permission for USF&S to mass-produce its patented waste containers under license.

I met with Copson and Kirch in Georgetown, where USF&S rents a suite of offices. They outlined what everyone agrees to be a real problem: commercial nuclear reactors produce huge amounts of spent fuel which contains plutonium, the material needed to produce nuclear weapons. An estimated 100,000 tons of spent fuel has piled up around the globe and no one has figured out a way to store it. The U.S. nuclear industry is looking to a site at the Yucca Mountains in Nevada, but Congress has yet to approve that site. Meanwhile, spent fuel is piling up at nuclear plants around the country. Similar problems exist in Russia—exacerbated by the fact that MinAtom is virtually bankrupt—and in all countries that produce nuclear power.

As outlined by Copson, the project's chief spokesman,

USF&S will lease uranium to nuclear reactor operators around the globe and deliver it to them with a fleet of 20 specially designed ships. The ships will return to pick up spent fuel rods from the nuclear plants and then transport the waste to a Pacific island, where it will be buried in containers weighing up to 110 tons. "Some people have billed us as anti-environmental, pro-nuclear, but it's really just the reverse," Copson says.

Copson calls USF&S a "pro-disarmament company" with a primary goal or preventing "rogue" countries like Iran and terrorist groups such as Hezbollah from obtaining the plutonium they need to build nuclear weapons: "The nuclear Visigoths are at the door, my friend. The only way to stop them is with us and this concept."

Others take a less sanguine view of the USF&S scheme. "The motivation for this plan is not world peace but dollars," said Patrick McGarey, an aide to Sen. Daniel Akaka of Hawaii, a leading opponent of USF&S. "If they are successful many people are going to get rich very fast." McGarey pointed out that USF&S plans to charge $1 million per ton in storage fees, which could generate billions of dollars for the company annually.

Greenpeace opposes cross-border movement of nuclear waste and believe countries that produce it should take responsibility for storing it. "There is still no proven technology that stores radioactive waste without eventually contaminating the environment," the group says.

Bullshit in the Pacific—and Washington

USF&S had an easy time lining up money and influence peddlers to back its plan. Finding a dump site proved more difficult. Like a crew of punch drunk sailors lost at sea, Murphy & Co. have desperately scouted the horizon for a Pacific Island where they can come aground. Copson explained to me that the Pacific was chosen because it lies between Russia and the

United States, and because it is littered with "useless dots of real estate." As he sees it, sacrificing a "tiny piece of bullshit in the Pacific" is a small price to pay in order to avoid the dooms-day scenario of nuclear annihilation.

USF&S circulated a 1994 feasibility study, labeled "CONFI-DENTIAL," that points to another reason why the company has been scouring the Pacific. The study noted that public confidence in nuclear safety had been "all but destroyed" by the near meltdown at Three Mile Island and the disaster at Chernobyl. As a result, all proposals to arrange for the storage of nuclear waste in the United States "have been met—and will continue to be met—by a firestorm of protest from state officials, public interest groups, and by those communities which would be affected." With "public resistance" high in Russia as well, "a solution may prove to be more readily achieved if the cooperation of a third country is successfully enlisted."

USF&S first approached the Marshall Islands, a former U.S. protectorate which entered into a "Compact of Free Association" with the U.S. upon becoming independent in 1986. The Defense Department used the Marshalls to conduct 23 nuclear tests during the early days of the Cold War. The biggest was in 1954, when the U.S. detonated the 15-megaton "Bravo Shot"—1,000 times more powerful than the bomb dropped on Hiroshima—on the Bikini atoll, a blast that exposed hundreds of Marshallese to radioactive fallout.

The feasibility study states that the Marshalls would make an "appropriate storage and disposal site" since some of the islands have already been rendered uninhabitable due to "vary-ing levels of residual radioactivity" from the Cold War era atomic tests. Another likely attraction (though one not men-tioned in the study) was that Murphy's son, Tom, is deputy chief of mission at the U.S. embassy in the Marshalls capital of Majuro.

A feudal system prevails in the Marshalls, which is ruled by King Amata Kabua. On October 14, 1994, the king received a fax from Murphy that laid out a preliminary proposal for a "global nuclear non-proliferation initiative." In exchange for "exclusive use of one suitable atoll" for nuclear storage, the plotters pledged to provide the king with $10 million up front and $50 million annually for three years as the project was implemented. After operations began, the Marshalls would receive further millions through a profit sharing arrangement.

Annual revenues for the King Kabua's government total about $70 million, and the large sums of money offered up by USF&S appear to have whetted the monarch's interest. However, fierce local resistance arose when word of the plan leaked to the public and the king decided to turn the deal down.

Copson took the rejection badly. "They're all scam artists, banging the tin cup in front of the white man," he later said of the Marshallese to a reporter from *Outside* magazine. "They'd open a whorehouse and sell their daughters and grandmothers for a dollar. They've never lived so good since that bomb, the fat lazy fucks."

Another possibility explored by USF&S was Midway Island, located 1,100 miles from Honolulu and site of a U.S. Navy base that the Pentagon had targeted for closing. In late 1995, Murphy wrote a letter to Navy Secretary name John Dalton asking for a long-term lease on the island. He promised that his company's plans to store vast quantities of nuclear waste there "would not disturb wildlife in the Midway habitat." To the dismay of USF&S, the Navy selected a competing bid from the U.S. Fish and Wildlife Service, which will run Midway as a nature preserve.

The next port of call was Palmyra, a tiny atoll about 1,000 miles south of Hawaii which is owned by the Fullard-Leo family of Honolulu but administered by the Department of the

Interior. USF&S drew up plans that showed that all the world's spent fuel could fit in the atoll's 5,400-acre lagoon, which would be filled with cement to prevent leakage.

Peter Savio, the Fullard-Leo's Honolulu-based real estate broker, said a Wall Street firm headed by Kirch, KVR, agreed to pay "in excess of $40 million" for Palmyra. "The buyers claimed they were interested in building a hotel and also mentioned plans for some sort of scientific research," he said. "They never discussed using the island as a nuclear waste site."

Once again, strong opposition to the plan arose when word leaked out about Murphy & Co's true intentions. The South Pacific Forum, an association of Pacific island governments that includes Australia and New Zealand, issued a statement that condemned the planned use of Palmyra as a "dumping ground for nuclear waste." Hawaii's congressional delegation soon entered the fray, with all six members signing a letter to President Clinton in June of 1996 urging him to oppose the project. "We question the wisdom of siting such a facility on an isolated atoll that is prone to erosion and extreme weather conditions," reads the letter. "Shipments of spent fuel and reprocessed nuclear materials by sea require extraordinary security measures. Even if careful precautions were observed, the safety of such cargo could not be guaranteed."

The death knell for the Palmyra plan came in August, when the White House sent Senator Akaka a letter promising that the Administration would "strongly oppose" the USF&S proposal. KVR then decided not to buy Palmyra, costing Kirch's firm what Savio termed a "substantial deposit."

Copson was as bitter about this setback as he was about the unraveling of the Marshalls plan. During our conversation he called Senator Akaka an "ignorant lightweight." McGarey, the senator's aide, would "realize the error of his ways when terrorists set off a bomb in Tel Aviv."

Undeterred by this latest setback, USF&S is focusing its

efforts on obtaining the use of Wake Island, site of a bloody World War II battle and now largely uninhabited. Wake is a major stopover for migratory birds and, like Midway, a wildlife refuge.

Policy over Wake is heavily influenced by a group of septua-genarian veterans mustered in the Wake Island Defenders Memorial Association. An internal budget proposal drawn up by USF&S shows that the company plans to buy the vets' sup-port with $500,000 annual contributions to the Memorial Association. The budget allocated $6 million for public rela-tions stunts to demonstrate the safety of the nuclear storage containers, which are to be subjected to "missile tests" and ramming by speeding trains.

The Politics of Pork

Though devoting much of their time to procuring a suitable piece of real estate, USF&S did not neglect the fine art of lob-bying. In 1996, it paid $60,000 to the firm of Oldaker, Ryan & Phillips—which also represents Philip Morris, Aetna, Ford and General Electric—to lobby for the dump. Grobmyer helped open doors with a few administration officials, but he failed to win a coveted face-to-face meeting with the president.

USF&S did, however, meet with Katie McGinty, director of the White House's Council on Environmental Quality, as well as officials from the Department of Energy, the Pentagon, the CIA and the National Security Council. A 1996 memoran-dum from Copson to the latter agency—"Subject: PREVENT-ING POLITICALLY UNSTABLE NATIONS BECOMING A NUCLEAR THREAT TO GLOBAL SECURITY"—said that USF&S had already held three meetings with MinAtom officials, who were "enthusiastic" about the plan. Copson, however, warned that time was of the essence and said that without "an unequivocal commitment by the U.S. government to support USF&S," the Russians might back off from their commitment to the deal.

Copson and other company officials also met with a number of important senators, including Majority Leader Trent Lott of Mississippi, Dale Bumpers of Arkansas, and Frank Murkowski of Alaska, chair of Senate Energy Committee. To pique their interest, USF&S offered a piece of the pork pie to all of these public servants. The company picked a Mississippi shipyards to build the specially designed ships to transport the nuclear waste. Storage containers were to be built in Arkansas and an Alaska company was selected to do construction work on Wake Island.

USF&S's lobbyists went so far as to draft legislation that would clear the way for their project. Titled the "Nuclear Disarmament Services Storage Facility Authorization Act of 1997," the bill would authorize the company to store up to 200,000 tons of nuclear waste on Wake Island. "In the interest of national security and to promote anti-terrorism," the bill would have waived sections of the Clean Water Act. For identical reasons, it would waive compliance with the National Environmental Policy Act, which would otherwise require the completion of an Environmental Impact Study before the government could authorize the project to move forward.

Copson and Kirch told me that the company had no intention of trying to sidestep environmental rules, and that the draft was intended purely for the Russians. "They're new to democracy and don't understand how it works," Copson said. "We drafted [the legislation] so we could show the Russians what a bill looks like."

Alas, Murphy & Co. had no more success in drumming up political support than they did in procuring a location to dump the nuclear refuse. No member of Congress stepped forward to press the company's cause on Capitol Hill and the Clinton administration refused to reconsider its earlier objections.

It could be that USF&S's problems had more to do with its failure to lubricate the gears of Washington than with the

If you enjoyed *Washington on $10 Million a Day,* you'll love *CounterPunch,* the exciting newsletter on power and evil in the capital that's written by Alexander Cockburn and Ken Silverstein.

Mail payment to
Counterpunch,
P.O. Box 18675
Washington, DC 20036

"Down and dirty muckracking..." *The Village Voice*

"The best political newsletter in the country...." *Out of Bounds*

"Badly needed..." Noam Chomsky

Yes, rush me my first issue of *CounterPunch!* I have enclosed this card with my check or money order for $40 ($25 low-income/senior/student) for a one-year subscription of 22 issues.

Name _____

Address _____

City _____ State _____ Zip _____

eccentricity of its endeavor. When Johnny Chung hoped to advance a number of bizarre schemes with the White House, including one to rescue a dissident from a Beijing jail, he forked over $366,000 to the Democrats in 1996 alone. When a group of right-wing Cubans wanted to hasten their plan to build an airport on a site that borders the Florida Everglades— a deal that may yet go forward—they unbuckled about $100,000 in campaign money.

USF&S's principals, on the other hand, were pikers. During the 1996 election campaign, only the hippie investment banker Kirch ponied up campaign cash and he offered a total of a paltry $900, all to the Democrats.

How a Little Lobbying Goes a Long Way

Many cases discussed in this chapter involve broad lobbying campaigns, fought over many years and on a variety of fronts, such as P&G's effort for olestra. However, much of the work performed by beltway lobbyists consists of hand-to-hand combat in the trenches of the political process, where a carefully worded addition to a major bill or a well crafted amendment can reap enormous benefits for one's client. (These battles generally take place far from public view.)

Lobbyists for Kenneth Mazik, head of the Au Clair School, a for-profit institution for poor children, won a huge windfall for their patron by expunging a single word from the 400-page welfare reform bill that passed Congress in 1996. Mazik's Delaware-based firm has a long record of abusing its wards. In the late-1970s, Mazik himself admitted to beating a mentally retarded boy with a riding crop, a practice he defended as therapeutic. In 1992, inspectors at one of Mazik's facilities found kids with unexplained broken noses, black eyes and missing teeth. Mazik was receiving $429 per day for the children, who were housed in trailers that smelled of feces and urine.

While Mazik skimped on expenditures for children, he spent liberally for lobbying the federal and state governments.

He was especially anxious to change a federal provision that allowed only non-profit institutions—which are generally acknowledged to provide better care than for-profit firms—to receive a variety of reimbursements from federal agencies.

Mazik's firm wined and dined child placement officials and state regulators at all-expense paid weekends in Florida. Company lobbyists met with members of Congress to argue the current rules discriminated against nonprofits and that the playing field needed to be leveled. In the end, Mazik's agents convinced Senator John Breaux of Louisiana to delete the word "nonprofit" from a single sentence in the welfare bill. With this one stroke, Au Clair and other for-profit firms became instantly eligible to receive millions of dollars in federal monies.

A more exuberant though equally discreet corporate porkfest occurred with another bill passed by Congress in 1996, legislation raising the minimum wage to $5.15 per hour (or a whopping total of $10,712 per year, based on a 40-hour work week.) In a billion-dollar giveaway to corporate raiders, the minimum wage bill allowed leveraged buyout specialists to take a tax deduction for fees they pay to investment banks and advisers. It also permitted newspaper publishers to treat distributors and carriers as independent contractors instead of employees, sparing publishers the burden of having to pay workers' social security benefits. "This is probably the best thing that has happened to the industry from a legislative standpoint in anyone's memory," John Sturm, president of the Newspaper Association of America, told *Editor and Publisher* at the time. The minimum wage bill killed off a surtax on diesel fuel for yachts and on luxury car purchases, and allowed Alaska seafood processors to deduct the cost of workers' meals.

Even as they larded the bill with corporate pork, Republicans in Congress tried to scale back the size of the increase in the minimum wage, allegedly the legislation's raison d'être. A big increase would "set off an inflationary spiral that will tax every American family," warned Rep. Robert Walker. Sen. Bob Dole—who pushed through the giveaway to newspaper publishers at the behest of the owners of the *Kansas City Star*—claimed that increasing the minimum wage would torpedo the economy. "Somebody's going to get hurt," Dole said in his inimitable fashion. "Somebody loses a job or closes up shop."

Meanwhile, President Clinton trumpeted the bill as evidence of his compassion for workers. "This is cause for celebration for all Americans of all parties, all walks of life, all faiths," he said upon signing the bill.

Beltway lobbyists must have had a good laugh over that line. The truth was that passage of the minimum wage bill had cost taxpayers $21 billion—in corporate freebies.

CHAPTER THREE

THE "PEOPLE SPEAK"

Grassroots and Front Groups

"If you can organize the grassroots, you could probably get a law passed saying the world's square."

—Ross Perot

Back in 1995, lobbyist Bob Beckel, campaign manager for Walter Mondale's 1984 presidential run and later founder of the Beckel Cowan lobby shop, was hired by the Competitive Long Distance Coalition, a group led by AT&T, MCI and Sprint. The coalition paid Beckel at least $2 million to drum up opposition to a bill that would allow the Baby Bells to compete with the big long distance carriers.

With the help of NTS, a Lynchburg, Virginia-based telemarketing firm, Beckel's campaign generated 500,000 telegrams to members of Congress. There was just one problem: up to half the telegrams were faked. Many were signed by people who had never heard of the bill. Other telegram senders turned out to be dead.

Indeed, the whole campaign was a fraud. NTS phoned people and asked if they were in favor of "competition" in telecommunications. If the response was affirmative, NTS asked if the person would like to send a telegram, at no cost, to his or her member of Congress. To heighten the impact of the drive, NTS sent out four telegrams per person. Twenty-seven House members wrote to the Competitive Long Distance

Coalition saying, "Our constituents have been manipulated, lied to and misrepresented...In our collective years of service none of us has ever before witnessed such reprehensible conduct."

Welcome to the brave new world of corporate grassroots lobbying, which has become the Fortune 500's favorite way to influence government policy. *Campaign and Elections* magazine reported in mid-1995 that some $790 million was spent on grassroots lobbying during the two previous years, a jump of 70 percent. Congress passed a lobbying reform bill in 1996, but conservatives succeeded in exempting disclosure requirements for "grassroots" lobbyists—who push legislation but don't personally meet with lawmakers—on the grounds that such restrictions would be a violation of free speech.

Though the practice has only recently taken off, the concept of corporate grassroots lobbying dates to the early 1970s. That period's student radicalism, along with the general political upheaval linked to Vietnam and Watergate, had shaken corporate leaders. In 1974 and 1975, The Conference Board, a business group which musters dozens of Fortune 500 firms, arranged a series of private discussions among top corporate officers. Comments at these meetings indicate that the assembled CEOs believed a Bolshevik uprising could be imminent: "Can we still afford one man, one vote? We are tumbling on the brink"; "We are terribly scared within this room. We are in serious trouble"; "Unless the press stops tearing down our system and begins to tell the public how it works, business leaders will not be permitted any future participation in the formation of social goals."

Out of such fears was born a carefully planned corporate campaign to recapture the culture. In 1973, some leading corporate executives formed the Business Roundtable. At the same time they breathed life into the moribund U.S. Chamber of Commerce, which quickly became a powerful lobbying force. But the polls they anxiously perused told business leaders that they were still viewed with great suspicion by the public. Therefore, they needed help from "independent" operations and scholars to lend a veneer of independent thinking about their concerns.

During the next decade, huge amounts of corporate money were deployed to establish a flurry of conservative think tanks, giving birth to big players such as the Cato Institute and the Heritage Foundation. Scores of lesser known research centers also sprang up, including Consumer Alert, a crusader for pesticides and nuclear energy; Citizens for the Sensible Control of Acid Rain, financed by electric utilities and coal companies; and the Princeton Dental Resource Center, paid for by M&M/Mars and the producer of a study a few years back that concluded that eating chocolate could be good for the teeth.

At the same time, but especially from the mid-1980s onward, the strategic philosophy of corporate lobbying was also shifting. Impressed by the organizing strength of unions, public interest groups and civil rights organizations, businesses began to emulate their techniques, giving rise to the new field of corporate "grassroots lobbying." To a large extent the model was Corporate America's hated foe, Ralph Nader.

Once a term that conjured up wholesome images of citizens spontaneously mustering to protect their interests, "grassroots lobbying" is now an industry directed by enormously expensive beltway consulting firms. The goal is to mime populist revolt. The phony grassrooters set up phone banks, manufacture letter-writing campaigns, arrange meetings between legislators and "white hat" community figures—preferably a religious leader or Little League coach—and rent "third party experts" to draft op-ed articles or testify before elected officials.

At a 1994 conference attended by dozens of corporate "grassroots specialists"—the meeting was titled "Shaping Public Opinion: If You Don't Do It, Somebody Else Will"—a public relations executive named Pamela Whitney claimed her outfit could parachute into a community and within two weeks "have an organization set up and ready to go." According to an account in the newsletter *PR Watch*, Whitney said that the key to success is looking local. To further that end, she hires local "ambassadors"—a woman who had been the head of the PTA was an ideal candidate. "It's important not to look like a Washington lobbyist. When I go to a zoning board meeting I wear absolutely no make-up, I comb my hair straight back in a ponytail, and I wear my kids' old clothes." A special added touch was donning a baseball cap.

Speaking to the same conference was John Davies of Davies Communications. His firm's literature claims that it "can make a strategically planned program look like a spontaneous explosion of community support." Davies explained how his telemarketers produce "personal" letters from real folks: "We want to assist them with letter writing. We get them on the phone, and while we're on the phone we say, 'Will you write a letter?' 'Sure.' 'Do you have the time to write it?' 'Not really.' 'Could we write the letter for you? I could put you on the phone right now with someone who could help you write a letter. Just hold, we have a writer standing by.' We hand-write it out on 'little kitty cat stationery' if it's an old lady. If it's a business we take it over to be photocopied on someone's letterhead. [We] use different stamps, different envelopes ... Getting a pile of personalized letters that have a different look to them is what you want to strive for."

Finally! A magazine for people who like to staple dogs!

In addition to arousing the masses, grassroots specialists also help companies with the dirty task of opposition research. *The Activist Reporter*, a magazine launched in 1995, promises to keep companies informed of pending "attacks by special interest groups" including environmentalists, shareholder "gadflies" and consumer safety advocates, as well as preparing company flacks for what to do when the media "come pounding on your client's door waving affidavits and copies of lawsuits, or holding press conferences denouncing their actions or products." Among the subscribers to the *Reporter*, which costs $195 for 12 monthly issues, are Coors Brewing Company, General Motors, Hewlett-Packard, Louisiana-Pacific, McDonald's and Raytheon.

A promo piece for the magazine warns that "when a crisis hits, there are precious few moments in which to prepare. Make the most of that time by having the information you need at your fingertips." Threats cited include "powerful environmental groups" that have accused companies like Boise-Cascade, Mitsubishi and Texaco of rain-forest destruction and global warming; animal-rights protests against the United States Surgical Corp.; and pressure applied by women's groups and minority activists against Denny's restaurants and Publix supermarkets "for their hiring practices, promotional policies and customer treatment."

Of course, these companies have well-deserved PR problems. Denny's settled claims over instances where African Americans were told to pay before eating, denied advertised specials and informed that the restaurant was closed when the doors were later opened to white customers. Florida-based Publix was the target of a class-action suit by woman employees, who say they were passed over for promotions and paid less than men. One worker, Melodee Shores, says she was told to "lose weight and put on make-up" if she wanted to be considered for a management position. United States Surgical faced boycotts over its policy of stapling live dogs, a threat company owner Leon Hirsch responded to by hiring spies to infiltrate an animal rights group.

No matter. With *The Activist Reporter*, subscribers get "concise reviews of a wide range of successful and failed public relations moves, strategies and crisis plans, allowing you to formulate your own playbook of preplanned actions."

Smoke, Mirrors and Populism:
Meet King of Astroturf Lobbying

Washington's leading corporate grassroots lobbyist is proba-bly Jack Bonner, a one-time legislative aide and press secretary to the late Sen. John Heinz of Pennsylvania. Bonner rents a suite of offices on 17th Street in downtown Washington, just off the "K" Street corridor, and has worked for bankers, drug makers, the steel industry, arms makers, insurance companies and the auto industry.

The heart of Bonner & Associates is its sophisticated tele-marketing operation, which Bonner once termed a "yuppie sweatshop." At any given time Bonner may have several hun-dred people working the phones on behalf of a handful of dif-ferent clients. "Bonner & Associates isn't a firm, it's a glorified phone bank," says one Washington lobbyist familiar with its operations.

All Bonner employees are required to sign a strict confiden-tiality agreement. When phoning, they are forbidden to reveal that they work for Bonner & Associates, a disclosure that would cast doubt on the authenticity of the grassroots drive.

Philip Morris hired Bonner in 1994 when the Occupational Safety and Health Administration (OSHA) issued a rule that would have restricted workplace smoking to rooms with sepa-rate ventilation systems. Bonner & Associates, which was paid $1.5 million for its work, sent a letter to small business owners urging them to write OSHA to oppose the regulation. Attached to the letter was a handy "checklist" of complaints to include in their correspondence. These included charges that the new rule would force businesses to "foot the tab for carry-ing out Washington's agenda" and that the cost of compliance would "divert resources otherwise available for payroll and jobs, thus increasing unemployment."

Bonner's work, along with similar "grassroots" campaigns run by R.J. Reynolds and other tobacco companies, produced the largest letter writing campaign in OSHA history, with 105,00 letters pouring in to the agency. The mountain of paperwork paralyzed OSHA, which was delayed from issuing a final rule on workplace smoking for more than four years.

Bonner also once helped the American Bankers Association (ABA) defeat an amendment which would have lowered astronomical interest rates charged by credit card companies. Bonner, who was reportedly paid $400,000 by the Bankers for his efforts, received a passionate "thank you" note from the group's executive vice president, Donald Ogilvie: "As you say in your ads: 'We help you win.' Well, speaking for the banking industry, you helped us win a big one. It was hard in several days to gain support for an issue that at first blush looked like a good idea to most people. After all, paying less interest on your credit cards sounds great. Nevertheless, Bonner & Assoc. achieved all of our goals."

When the Going Gets Tough, Recruit the Boy Scouts

One of Bonner's fortes is enlisting "white hats" to promote his clients' legislative priorities, thereby allowing the client to remain discreetly hidden from public view. As Bonner—who refused my request for an interview—once explained, "Some guy in a pinstripe suit telling a senator this bill is going to hurt Pennsylvania doesn't have the impact of someone in Pennsylvania saying it."

Auto makers once hired Bonner to oppose an amendment which required the Big Three to build smaller, more fuel-efficient cars. To oppose this seemingly unobjectionable measure, Bonner called upon the elderly and the physically handicapped, who have a hard time getting into smaller cars with walkers, wheelchairs and other special equipment. He also roped in volunteer organizations that ferry around members in large vehicles, as well as police chiefs, who feared the bill would result in large police cruisers being replaced by tiny Toyotas.

Bonner flew in the head of the South Dakota Easter Seals, a top official from a Florida seniors group and Boy Scout representatives to attend a D.C. press conference. Confronted by such opposition, Congress swiftly crumbled; the amendment died in committee.

In 1996, the American Sugar Alliance retained Bonner to fight off a Congressional effort to reduce government subsidies for the sugar industry, a leading recipient of corporate welfare. For this effort, Bonner lined up support from such wholesome groups as the Detroit Association of Black Organizations, the Mideast Baptist Conference and the Allegheny Labor Council. After the battle was won, Alliance Chairman Luther Markwart wrote Bonner to thank him for helping beat back "one of the toughest legislative challenges in the history of the industry." Victory was achieved, Markwart wrote, "because of the well-briefed and high quality of the grassroots supporters who made the initial calls, as well as the overall management of the calls by your staff."

One problem for Bonner and other "grassroots" practitioners is that their techniques are increasingly easy to spot by congressional staffers. An aide to one congressman who Bonner & Associates targeted on the sugar issue said that during House debate on the bill his boss's district office suddenly began receiving stacks of unsigned form letters in favor of sugar subsidies. "When it comes in bunches you can recognize it as Astroturf," said the staffer. "It's not taken very seriously."

As a result, Bonner & Associates strives to develop tactics that are harder to recognize as bogus. One innovative strategy used by the firm is to fax letters of support to people won over during a phone conversation, have them sign their name inside a black box on the page, and fax it back to Bonner's office. His firm then scans the signature into a computer and transposes it on to a petition that is sent to lawmakers. Petitions contain signatures from a set geographic location, so recipients in Congress are hopefully deluded into thinking that they were forwarded by a constituent who stood out on a street corner or shopping mall as part of a genuine grassroots campaign.

Bonner Turns Up the Heat for the Coal Industry

Over the summer of 1997, Bonner was hired by a coal industry front group called the Western Fuels Association. His task was to mobilize opposition to a modest proposal from the Clinton administration to combat global warming by reducing emissions of carbon dioxide (CO_2), which are produced by fossil fuels such as coal, oil and gasoline.

The business community is split on the issue of global warming. Companies such as Dow Chemical, General Electric and United Technologies have endorsed the administration's position. A coalition of natural gas companies has positioned itself to the left of the Clinton administration, saying that the U.S. can cut back greenhouse emissions faster than the president proposes (by shifting, of course, to use of more natural gas).

The coal industry, meanwhile, rabidly opposes any attempts to reduce greenhouse gases and insists that there is no consensus that CO_2 contributes to global warming. In fact, some 2,600 top scientists have signed a statement that supports the linkage, while less than a dozen dissidents argue to the contrary. Among the latter are Dr. Patrick Michaels of the University of Virginia, whose work has been financed by Western Fuels and the German Coal Mining Association, and S. Fred Singer, who is supported by Exxon, Shell, ARCO and Sun Myung Moon's Unification Church. Singer hasn't published a peer reviewed article for more than twenty years.

If Bonner's phone script for Western Fuels is to be believed, only the most deranged tree huggers could possibly favor limits on CO_2 emissions. "Hello, my name is _____, and I'm calling you about a public policy issue that will directly and direfully affect your members," it begins. "This issue could cause your members to pay a lot more for the basic necessity of electricity that they use at home and work. Additionally, it could put many Americans out of work." The campaign targeted "grasstops" leaders—mostly heads of business and community groups—who were told that the campaign's goal was to help out "farmers, small businesses, seniors and the poor."

After discussing the dire economic consequences of any crackdown on fossil fuels, the script goes on to describe CO_2 as a "benign gas that is good for forests, plant life, and agriculture." A fact sheet used by Bonner & Associates employees further explained that "the world's scientists are divided" as to whether carbon dioxide is harmful to the environment. "Some scientists theorize, based on computer guessing, that the CO_2 released into the air adversely affects global warming and the global climate," telemarketers are trained to say. "Other scientists have conducted research with computer models and suggest that this is not a significant problem."

At the end of their pitch, Bonner & Associates employees asked targets to sign an "open letter" to President Clinton on the topic. The letter urged the president to rethink support for his administration's "anti-family" global warming proposal.

I called the toll-free number listed on the telephone script for the Western Fuels campaign and claimed that an uncle in Iowa, a state targeted by the campaign, had already been contacted by a telemarketer about the global warming issue and had urged me to call in to see what I could do to help out. "Legislative Hotline," answered the woman who took my call. She hemmed and hawed when I asked who she worked for, finally saying, "We just deal with whatever the current legislative issues are." After thanking me for calling—"It's important that people are aware of these issues"—this person put me through to a Pam Seidel, who was identified as the head of the Western Fuels campaign.

After I again explained why I was calling, Seidel told me that "many scientists" are not convinced of the danger posed by global warming. "The U.S. already spends $29 billion a year on pollution control," she said—failing to mention that it is still the largest producer of greenhouse gases, with per capita emissions twenty times higher than second place China. "That's why we want the president and Congress to take another look" at the issue.

At the end of our brief discussion I asked Seidel who she worked for. "I represent Western Fuels," she said. "Our main office is in Lakewood, Colorado. We have another in Wyoming and I'm in the office in Arlington, Virginia." Western Fuels does have an office in Arlington but when I called I was told that no Pam Seidel worked there. There is, however, a Pam Seidel on staff at Bonner & Associates in downtown Washington.

Western Fuels has dabbled in grassroots campaigning in the past. Back in 1991 it helped form the Information Council on the Environment (ICE), whose goal, according to internal documents, was to "reposition global warming as theory (not fact)." It sought to target "older, less educated males from larger households who are not typically active information seekers," and "younger, lower-income women." ICE's campaign was scratched when its strategic blueprint was leaked to the press.

The themes crafted by ICE were pressed into service by Bonner & Associates. In addition to emitting the "benign gas" carbon dioxide, coal creates nearly 100,000 jobs per year, claimed Bonner's callers, and "makes America independent of unreliable foreign energy suppliers." Reducing greenhouse emissions, on the other hand, would be "bad for America." It would "reduce American wages each year by 5% to 10%," cause the price of electricity to skyrocket and "devastate and wipe out major U.S. industries and employers, including large American employers such as the steel industry, the paper industry, and the aluminum industry."

Because much of its electricity comes from coal-fired plants, Bonner's phoners targeted Iowa for the warm and fuzzy carbon dioxide campaign. Western Fuels used signatures they collected in a full-page advertisement it placed in the *Des Moines Register* under the heading "OPEN LETTER TO THE CONGRESS, PRESIDENT CLINTON, AND VICE PRESIDENT GORE." The ad declared that stiffening emission standards on greenhouse gases would result in families being "forced to pay much more for the basic necessity of electricity," and complained that "many scientists cannot agree that global warming is a real and significant problem."

Eighteen signatures accompanied the text. Most were business leaders, such as Sharon Presnall of the Iowa Bankers Association and Matt Eide from the Iowa Association of Business and Industry. A few labor officials signed as well, including Roger Boyles of the local Carpenter's Union in Cedar Rapids, who was listed in the ad as representing 550 carpenters. In a phone interview Boyles said he had a vague recollection of signing a statement—which he faxed to Bonner's office where his signature was scanned onto the ad—that had something to do with "changes in the environment" that might cost union members their jobs. Upon hearing that the Western Fuels campaign was being run out of a beltway lobby shop, Boyles said, "That would kind of flat piss me off."

Another union signer was Len Hersh of the Operating Engineers of Iowa City. Like Boyles, he was upset to learn about Bonner & Associates's role in the campaign. "I didn't realize it was a big lobbying group," he said. "Maybe I'm realizing a guy got duped a little."

One person not taken in by Bonner's hustlers was Dave Jones of the Cedar Rapid Painter's Union, who said two people—both who identified themselves as working for Western Fuels's Colorado office—called him about twenty times and pressed him to sign the ad. He was intrigued by the pitch because it had a consumer angle, but refused to sign on to the campaign because he had never heard of Western Fuels and was suspicious of the phoners' integrity. "They were soliciting signers to their position without adequately explaining what they were signing on to," Jones realized. "They're trying to manipulate people by phone to influence public opinion in the state of Iowa."

I also secured materials documenting Bonner's involvement in the battle over deregulation of the utilities industry. This is not an issue on which it is easy to choose sides. Proponents of deregulation, led by natural gas giant Enron, want Congress to break up utility monopolies. The "deregulators" have created a number of front groups, including the Electricity Consumer's Resource Council, with the consumers in question being Fortune 500 firms such as Amoco, Shell, Monsanto, General Motors, Procter & Gamble, Ford and DuPont.

Among those opposing the deregulators is a Bonner client, the Electric Utility Shareholders Alliance (EUSA). Though depicting itself as a humble, folksy group that represents "individual investors holding millions of shares of utility company stock," EUSA is dominated by big utility companies—members include Commonwealth Edison, Carolina Power & Light and Hawaiian Electric Industries—seeking to maintain their monopoly position. EUSA's four-member "national advisory committee" includes Edward Rissing, a Bonner & Associates vice president and a former lobbyist for the Edison Electric Institute (EEI), the trade group for utility companies. Two other members of the advisory committee also have links to the utilities industry, as does EUSA's chairman, William Steinmeier, a former Missouri utility regulator and consultant whose clients included Edison Electric.

For a 1997 campaign, Bonner's sweatshop operators sent their targets a letter—on EUSA letterhead and with the words

"Grassroots Effort" prominently displayed in the upper left hand corner—which burns with populist fervor. It urged them to "stand up to the big corporations" pushing utility deregulation," and warns that if they don't act, the "big boys in Washington" will determine policy on electricity, instead of "the folks in your state."

The letter was signed by Randal Joyner, who is identified as EUSA's "Regional Grassroots Coordinator." As one phone call revealed, Joyner actually works at Bonner & Associates beltway headquarters.

Recipients were asked to sign a second letter that accompanies the dispatch from Joyner. Addressed to "Members of Congress," the letter describes proponents of deregulation as "powerful, well-connected special interests" and urges Congress to "stand up to the giant corporations" who are promoting deregulatory legislation. The letter further states that deregulation will "hurt the environment—especially the air we breathe." Bonner's deployment of this argument would likely come as a nasty shock to the Western Fuels Association. Deregulation would indeed be harmful to the environment because it would encourage utility companies to bring on-line more coal-fired plants, which are cheaper to operate but unfortunately produce CO_2—which while working for one client is "good for forests, plant life, and agriculture," but which here is acknowledged to be a gross pollutant.

Bonner and other "grassroots" lobbyists claim that all they do is mobilize the citizenry to take part in the political process. But as one Washington lobbyist who formerly worked for the AFL-CIO says of Bonner, "It's easy to manipulate people and his [phoners] know exactly what buttons to push. By the time they're done you're saying, 'Yeah, that's an effort I want to be a part of!' Jack's not informing people to strengthen democracy. He just uses them and discards them after they've served their purpose."

Tort Reform: The Corporate Agenda

While Bonner & Associates' grassroots humbuggery largely consists of phone work, other beltway lobby shops make use of a more diverse set of tools in promoting Corporate America's legislative ambitions. One such firm is APCO Associates, whose billing fees hit $12.7 million in 1996, up 24 percent from the previous year. The company provides a broad variety of services to its corporate clientele, including direct lobbying of Congress, coordinating strategic philanthropic activities, and handling "crisis management." APCO's promotional literature even pledges to monitor "emerging grassroots efforts that might lead to or result in negative actions affecting clients (such as boycotts or regulatory actions)."

But grassroots lobbying—which it calls "political support services"—is APCO's specialty. "[We employ] campaign tactics to create an environment in support of our client's legislative and regulatory goals," says an APCO brochure. "Our staff has written the direct mail, managed the telephones [and] crafted the television commercials."

APCO's clients are mostly Fortune 500 firms, including a variety of tobacco makers, drug companies and insurance firms. They pay APCO to set up bogus "independent" coalitions without apparent links to industry. "You won't read about APCO on the front page of a newspaper talking about our work, but that doesn't mean that our work isn't making the front page," reads the promotional brochure. "We're proud of our record and we're even prouder that [the media writes] about our campaigns and their results—not us."

One of APCO's creations is The Advancement of Sound Science Coalition (TASSC), whose chairman is Garrey Carruthers, the conservative former governor of New Mexico. Its board includes Clayton Yeutter, the former U.S. Trade Representative and now a lobbyist at Hogan and Hartson, and Michael Fumento, a resident fellow at the American

Enterprise Institute.

TASSC's stated aim is to combat the "consequences of inappropriate science through focusing attention on current examples of unsound government research used to guide policy decisions." The real agenda of the corporations that fund TASSC is to oppose any safety or health regulations that might impinge on their bottom line. One coalition publication stated that American agriculture is being undermined by the "exaggerated public fears over pesticides" that environmentalists have stirred up.

Members of this preposterous "public interest" group regularly write op-ed articles and TASCC itself is treated with great reverence by the press. The *Denver Post* called it an organization that provides "a much needed balance to the public debate that often surrounds disputed areas of science."

APCO also helped create the Washington, D.C.-based American Tort Reform Association, which is leading the nationwide campaign for "tort reform." This soothing term masks a business-backed campaign that would shield corporations from product liability lawsuits arising from their sale of dangerous and defective products, such as tobacco, asbestos and the Dalkon Shield birth control device.

ATRA says in a fund-raising letter that it is "not a wealthy special-interest group backed by vast cash resources...ATRA is the homeowner tired of paying exorbitant insurance premiums for minimal coverage. ATRA is the average citizen looking for an end to the threat of being sued." But lurking behind the scenes at ATRA are big business groups which have a direct stake in curbing product liability lawsuits. Among the more conspicuous are insurance companies, drug manufacturers, tobacco companies and pharmaceutical firms.

The chief target of ATRA are trial lawyers, who are portrayed in Association literature as mercenaries who will file even the most frivolous lawsuit in the hopes of collecting a big contingency fee. Trial lawyers, in fact, can often make for a juicy target.

But the liability limiters' true concerns are revealed in the case of Pfizer's Bjork-Shiley heart valve, which killed at least 750 people worldwide and was still knocking off recipients at a rate of one to three per month until at least 1994. Pfizer learned about problems with the valve shortly after putting it on the market in 1979 but sought to keep defects hidden, even writing the FDA to urge the agency "not to notify the public." By the time an FDA investigation forced the company to take the valve off the market in 1986, Pfizer had racked up some $100 million in profits. Under legislation pushed by ATRA and its allies, Bjork-Shiley victims would have had sharply limited grounds to sue because the FDA had approved the valve (though based on insufficient data from Pfizer).

While ATRA maintains its own staff and offices, the "tort reform" campaign is coordinated from APCO's offices. The strategy of APCO Vice President Neal Cohen—who ATRA lists as its "grass-roots consultant"—is to take the complex issue of tort law and reduce it to a question of lawsuit abuse. Under his direction, APCO prepared a series of television spots, print ads and in-flight videos for air travelers. In one TV ad, firefighters complain that they're so fearful of lawsuits that they hesitate to rescue people in burning buildings. In fact, since almost all firefighters work for governmental agencies, they can't be sued.

Democracy for Corporations, 101

Cohen is keenly aware of the need to keep his firm's clients out of the limelight, as this would detract from the illusion that the "tort reform" outfits arise from a spontaneous, local explosion by outraged citizens and small businesses. In 1994, Cohen was a star speaker at a conference on corporate grassroots lobbying held at the Colony Beach & Tennis Resort in Sarasota, Florida. Cohen warned his colleagues—who included representatives from State Farm, Schering-Plough, the American Council of Life Insurance, Nationwide Insurance, and Southwestern Bell—that opponents of tort reform would go after some of the movement's biggest backers, such as insurance companies, chemical firms and pharmaceutical makers:

> You need to have credibility and that means when you pick people to join your coalition, make sure they're credible. And if they're not credible, keep 'em away. In a tort reform battle, if State Farm—I think they're here—Nationwide, is the leader of the coalition, you're not going to pass the bill. It's not credible. Because it's so self-serving; everybody knows that the insurance companies would be one beneficiary... You've got to make sure the leaders of the coalition are credible, and the core group of the coalition and the spokespeople...

> If you contribute big money to a coalition you better be at the table when the decisions are made and...it ought to be a card table and not a corporate [board room] table. Broad-based membership is: 'What does the public see? What do the legislators see? Decision-making is: a core group of three or so people who have similar interests and who are going to get the job done.'

Cohen and APCO chieftain Marjorie Krause boast in private that they coined the term "junk lawsuit." In his warmly received address to the Public Affairs Council, he states that "Rule No. 1 for me is stay away from substance. Don't talk about the details of legislation. Talk about...frivolous lawsuits, lawsuit abuse, trial lawyer greed."

Cohen has been central to creating a host of Astroturf groups at the state level, typically called Citizens Against Lawsuit Abuse. To aid these outfits, APCO conducts extensive polling, pays "independent" academics to prepare handy research papers, runs phone banks and otherwise oversees the operations of the state chapters.

In Mississippi, where APCO in 1993 dreamed up

Mississippians for a Fair Legal System (MFFLS), Cohen gloated that weak disclosure laws meant that opponents "didn't really know [which business interests were] at the heart of everything. The problem they faced was we had 1,500 Mississippians mixed in with who our clients were." He also boasted that the MFFLS had recruited Warren Hood, owner of one of the state's biggest banks and the one which politicians often relied on for campaign loans. This, he exclaimed, made Hood someone elected officials found especially hard to say "no" to.

Cohen is not eager to discuss APCO's activities outside of the cozy confines of a corporate PR conference. When I called him to ask if APCO worked for tobacco companies, he said, "It's a firm policy to never reveal who our clients are unless it's a public requirement." He brought the interview to a hasty close after I informed him that I had secured a tape of his conference remarks.

Smoke Screen

The tobacco industry is one of the foremost practitioners of corporate grassroots lobbying, a fact that's not surprising. As the industry is held in such low esteem by the public, its lobbyists shun the spotlight, instead hiding behind a web of hired front groups, think tanks and grassroots specialists.

Among the more brazenly named tobacco front groups is the Oakland, California-based Independent Institute, which has received tens of thousands of dollars from both Philip Morris and R.J. Reynolds. The institute subsequently published a study called "Sin Taxes: The Political Consequences of Incorrect Behavior," which opposed excise taxes on cigarettes.

With the help of Burson-Marsteller, Philip Morris also set up the National Smokers Alliance. The alliance has an annual budget of roughly $11 million, of which some $7 million is provided by the tobacco maker. At one point the NSA was headed by Thomas Humber, who at the time was a vice president of Burson-Marsteller. "In order to recruit new members, the NSA sends recruits into bars, bowling alleys, bingo parlors and country fairs to sign up members, and pays a commission for each," reads an internal 1996 report on tobacco lobbying prepared by State Affairs, a PR firm that works for Philip Morris. "Currently, membership is 1 million smokers, and the NSA runs advertisements in Washington publications, distributes a newsletter, collects signatures on petitions for pro-smoking ballot initiatives and lobbies against smoking restrictions imposed by state and local governments."

The tobacco barons have also played a vibrant if discreet role in the "tort reform" movement. Thanks to its vast resources and squads of lobbyists, tobacco has, as of this writing, never paid out a penny in a product liability suit. However, the legal immunity enjoyed by tobacco firms—whose chief product, cigarettes, kill roughly 450,000 every year—has grown ever more precarious.

Until the early 1980s, the tobacco industry was essentially immune from civil liability through the legal doctrine of "assumption of risk." If a consumer used a product that was known to be dangerous, he or she was deemed to have full responsibility for any and all consequences.

The tobacco companies have long recognized that their legal shelter might one day be eroded. As far back as 1970, a lawyer from British American Tobacco (BAT), owner of Brown & Williamson, acknowledged in an internal memo that the company "for some time [has] been concerned over the possibility that the BAT might in the future be involved in smoking and health litigation in the USA."

By the mid-1980s, alarm bells were ringing at tobacco headquarters. A June 17, 1984 memo from J.K. Wells, corporate counsel for BAT, reported that the company's legal team feared that "changes in U.S. product liability law, aggressiveness of plaintiffs' lawyers, and smoking health sciences since the

1960s...have rendered product liability actions against the manufacturers more difficult to defend in the 1980s." Wells fretted that "adverse evidence which could be attributed to the defendants is a serious problem" and that "papers produced by BAT on smoking and health for internal and worldwide distribution" could be introduced as evidence at trial.

The following year Brown & Williamson and two other tobacco firms, Philip Morris and Lorillard, hired Arnold & Porter to help prepare an early line of defense against the threat of product liability lawsuits. Arnold & Porter promptly retained public relations specialist John Scanlon, who, according to a 1987 article in *Playboy*, began collecting "newspaper clippings from across the country concerning outrageous claims in personal-injury cases." These stories were then sent to influential reporters, columnists, editors and TV producers.

"There was very little chance of being able to turn the public's mind around on the issue of smoking," Scanlon told the magazine. "But start, as I did, with the proposition that most of these liability cases are a demonstrable effect of the increase in the number of lawyers in America. Then try to generate a body of data about lawyers' excesses that the public can easily understand. My clients could only be the beneficiaries of that kind of consciousness." Helped along by the insurance industry, Scanlon's efforts bore fruit. Soon, the media reflected the anguished cries of business leaders who complained that a "tort explosion" was undermining Corporate America.

While the industry scored victories on the public relations front, the legal situation of the tobacco companies was becoming ever more precarious. Thousands of documents leaked from the companies have shown that the tobacco barons have known for decades that nicotine is addictive. Just as damaging were reams of documents which revealed the industry's efforts to target kids.

A 1969 Philip Morris memo said that most people start

smoking between ages of 16 and 20 and continue because of "the pharmacological effect of smoke upon the body of the smoker," which at times is so powerful that the need for a tobacco fix "preempts food in times of scarcity on the smoker's priority list." Another company memo from more than two decades later called cigarettes a "nicotine delivery system" and likened nicotine to cocaine.

In 1973, R.J. Reynolds's assistant director of research, Claude Teague, Jr., drafted a memo discussing how the company could most effectively hook young people. "The smoking-health controversy does not appear important to [teenagers] because, psychologically, at eighteen, one is immortal," Teague wrote. "Thus, a new brand aimed at the young group should not in any way be promoted as a 'health' brand, and perhaps should carry some implied risk. In this sense, the warning label on the package may be a plus."

These revelations have strengthened cases by plaintiffs who charge that they became addicted to nicotine at a very early age and were unable to stop as adults. Therefore, it is argued, they did not make a free choice to become smokers and there was no assumption of risk.

Furthermore, assumption of risk clearly does not apply to victims of second-hand smoke. In a major blow to the tobacco lords, a Florida appeals court ruled in January of 1996 that a group of airline flight attendants could mount a national class-action suit against tobacco companies over precisely this issue.

Richard Daynard, chairman of the Tobacco Product Liability Project says the new generation of tobacco lawsuits "will be aided by abundant new evidence of industry wrongdoing...The tobacco companies will no longer be seen as honest purveyors of a legal product...They will be seen, rather, as dishonest pushers of an unregistered (and hence illegal) drug called nicotine."

That assessment was mirrored in a 1993 report from M.J.

Whitman Investment Research. It warned investors to be wary of holding any tobacco-related securities and predicted that lawsuits against the industry "will grow in number, ultimately rivaling asbestos personal injury cases in industry impact."

Gimme Shelter: Why Tobacco Backs Tort Reform

All of this has given tobacco plenty of incentive to back the tort reform campaign (though, as always, the industry has desperately sought to remain far from the spotlight). The influence of tobacco on the campaign is seen in the membership roster of ATRA. Among the companies that pay the bills at ATRA—in addition to Aetna, Boeing, Exxon, General Electric and Pfizer—are Philip Morris, Brown & Williamson and Universal Leaf & Tobacco, a company which supplies tobacco to cigarette companies. At least one of ATRA's top directors, Samuel B. Witt, III, has links to tobacco as well. He formerly served as an executive and attorney for R.J. Reynolds and for a period directed the company's product liability efforts in the states.

In recent years, ATRA and its allies have scored victories in more than a dozen states and "reform" legislation is pending in many others. An article in the *ABA Journal* in August of 1995 said that while Congress still hadn't acted on a federal product liability bill, "the states may already have done the job."

While the tobacco barons have generally sought to cover their tracks, the industry's links to these statewide movements are easy to find. Tobacco scored a big victory in California in 1987, when the state trial lawyers cut a deal with the Association for California Tort Reform—a group funded by R.J. Reynolds and Philip Morris—and pushed through the "Civil Liability Reform Act." That bill made it almost impossible to sue makers of "inherently unsafe" products such as butter, sugar, alcohol and cigarettes. The act's language was crafted by Richard Kingham of D.C.-based Covington & Burling, a firm that represents the Tobacco Industry and Philip Morris.

Covington & Burling also played a leading role in a huge but ultimately unsuccessful tort reform effort in Pennsylvania. Kingham and another firm lawyer helped set up the Pennsylvania Task Force on Product Liability, which mustered some of the nation's leading corporations, including British American Tobacco and Philip Morris, the latter which was one of the group's top funders.

The lawyers helped write the task force's proposed legislation, which would have prohibited suits against manufacturers more than 15 years after a product was sold and also contained a clause which exempted from prosecution manufacturers of "common consumer products" known to be risky. In addition to Kingham—who concedes that he has also pressed for liability limits in Ohio, New Jersey, Texas and Indiana—at least twenty more tobacco lobbyists were deployed to press for the measure.

Sen. David Brightbill supported the liability limiters bill but sought to strip the clause that offered legal protection to the tobacco lords. Though proponents insisted that the bill's purpose was not to protect tobacco, they voted down the Brightbill amendment (thereby generating suspicion about their motives and ultimately helping defeat the bill).

In Texas, a 1993 tort reform bill passed by the state legislature prohibits lawsuits in the case of "common consumer product[s] intended for personal consumption, such as sugar, castor oil, alcohol, tobacco, and butter." The measure was modeled on California's 1987 law, and, like in that case, resulted from a deal struck between trial lawyers and a business lobby.

Tobacco lobbyists were at the forefront of the movement, which was led by the Texas Civil Justice League (TCJL). A key player was Jack Gullahorn of the law firm of Akin, Gump, who headed Philip Morris's state product liability team in the early 1990s and who was also paid by the TCJL—between $10,000 and $25,000 according to financial disclosure reports—for his efforts on behalf of "reform" (more recently, Gullahorn has lobbied for the NRA and U.S. Tobacco). Two other Philip Morris lobbyists, Rusty Kelley and Buddy Jones, were also central to the tort reform battle.

In 1994, tort reformers launched a major drive in New Jersey—where tobacco had already won substantial protection in 1987—that was led by one of the CALA groups set up by APCO. CALA's literature described the group as being comprised of hundreds of small businesses, neglecting to mention that it received major financial support from the tobacco industry (and from Bristol-Myers Squibb, which was facing suits for its silicone breast implants, and Owens-Corning Fiberglass, the manufacturer of asbestos).

In fact, CALA was based in the offices of Princeton Public Affairs, a firm headed by Dale Florio, Philip Morris's top New Jersey lobbyist. Not only had Florio formerly been director of Philip Morris's state government affairs operations, but the tobacco company had paid to put him through law school. Though he had no formal affiliation with CALA, Florio ran the outfit and the overall tort reform campaign. For his efforts, Philip Morris paid him $300,000 between 1994 and 1995. Three other major tobacco companies, American Brands, Brown & Williamson, and Lorillard, tossed in $24,000 each.

Also working on the campaign was John Sheridan, whose law firm of Riker, Danzig, Scherer, Hyland & Perretti represents R.J. Reynolds. It was Sheridan who had drafted the 1987 law which barred most suits against tobacco companies, a task he performed while on retainer for Covington & Burling. His fees were picked up by, among others, Philip Morris and RJR.

Burning Cash

At the federal level, the tort reformers have also been making headway. With the Republican seizure of Congress in 1994, tobacco companies and other liability limiters believed they had their best chance ever to push through a business-friendly bill. The incoming head of the House Commerce Committee was Rep. Tom Bliley of Virginia, long an intimate friend of the tobacco firms and representing a district whose biggest private employer is Philip Morris. He replaced Rep. Henry Waxman of California, one of the industry's fiercest foes in Congress.

The tobacco barons had the foresight to stuff the coffers of the Republican National Committee with more than $600,000 in soft money during the 1993 to 1994 election cycle, making the industry one of the party's biggest donors. In a letter to stockholders in early 1995, Philip Morris CEO Geoffrey Bible wrote that "new faces and new leadership on Capitol Hill [give us] tremendous opportunities to get new and unbiased hearings on the issues that concern us most."

Pleasantly sated with money from tobacco and other tort reform backers, Congress passed a product liability bill in 1996 that would have capped damages at $250,000, even in cases where a company had lied about the dangers posed by its product (that figure, incidentally, is about 3 percent of the 1994 earnings—$7.8 million—of Geoffrey Bible of Philip Morris). Other changes proposed by Congress include a "loser pays" provision that would discourage plaintiffs from initiating a case against well-heeled industries such as tobacco, since the potential cost to the loser would be enormous; and a "statute of repose," which would bar lawsuits 15 years after "the date of delivery of the product involved to its first purchaser." Since most tobacco-related diseases take 20 years or more to develop, this would slam the door on the plaintiffs in any smoker addiction lawsuits.

President Clinton caused much surprise by vetoing the bill passed by Congress. The veto should not be interpreted as a sign of populist inflammation on the part of the Man from Hope. The Association of Trial Lawyers of America is the foremost opponent of the product liability bill. It is also one of the biggest contributors to the Democratic Party and lavishly funded the president's re-election campaign.

Tort reform will be back on Congress's plate soon and with Clinton not running for re-election, business will have a better chance of getting a bill signed into law. Just in case, the tobacco lords have been seeking to negotiate a deal with a group of state attorney generals, 40 of whom are suing tobacco companies to recover Medicaid costs linked to treating smoking-related illnesses. The deal would require the tobacco companies to pay out about $350 billion over 25 years, some which would be used to pay compensatory damage to smokers. At the same time, the proposal (at least as it stood in late 1997, as Congress was still considering the deal), would shield the tobacco lords from future product liability lawsuits. It would also allow them to continue to sell abroad, where the industry makes an ever-increasing share of its profits.

Big Tobacco's Lapdog Watchdog

During the summer of 1996, a new beltway watchdog group, Contributions Watch, released a report on the amount of money trial lawyers have donated to federal candidates. The study received extensive coverage, including a story in the *Wall Street Journal* and a lengthy cover article in Rupert Murdoch's *Weekly Standard*. The latter article, written by Carolyn Lochhead, Washington correspondent for the *San Francisco Chronicle*, called the report from the "nonprofit" Contributions Watch a "major breakthrough" that revealed trial lawyers to be the "most powerful special interest group in the U.S."

But this study was no disinterested piece of research and Contributions Watch was not an "independent, national research organization committed to examining the amount of special interest money that flows to candidates," as it claimed in the introduction to the trial lawyer report. As I learned from company documents leaked by a disgruntled employee, Contributions Watch was created and controlled by the State

Affairs Company, a powerful beltway lobby shop. The "independent" study on trial lawyers was bought and paid for by Philip Morris and the tobacco industry as part of its unceasing campaign for tort reform. State Affairs even billed Philip Morris for planting the reports in the *Journal* and the *Standard*.

Contributions Watch marked a new step in the debasement of the political system by the Fortune 500. Corporations have moved beyond merely setting up bogus "grassroots" organizations to back their legislative goals. Now they're establishing their own "watchdog" groups.

State Affairs is a PR and lobby shop staffed with players from the beltway's bipartisan political establishment. The firm's partners include:

- David McCloud, former chief of staff to Virginia Senator Charles Robb and a past senior vice president of Burson Marsteller.

- Bobby Watson, a former advisor to Robb, ex-chief operating officer for the Democratic National Committee and a member of the Clinton/Gore "rapid response team" during the 1992 campaign.

- Charles Francis, formerly at Burson-Marsteller, Hill & Knowlton and Chase Manhattan Bank, where he was a speech writer for David Rockefeller.

- John Davis, a Republican who has worked as a campaign adviser to Bob Dole and to former Tennessee Senator Howard Baker.

- William Timmons, who has worked for the Republican National Committee and the National Republican Senatorial Committee.

These are not only heavy hitters but notoriously dirty hitters as well. McCloud and Watson both resigned from Robb's staff after pleading guilty to charges involving an illegal wiretap of Virginia Governor Douglas Wilder, one of Robb's political enemies. To collect information on the trial lawyers for State Affairs, McCloud's son, Patrick, infiltrated the American Trial Lawyers Association by posing as a law student.

State Affairs's clients—who pay billing rates of $200 per hour for partners and $150 per hour for associates—include Citicorp, Blue Cross/Blue Shield, the National Firearms Association, Wells Fargo Bank and Bering Fisheries, as well as the Democratic National Committee. The firm's biggest cash cow, however, is the tobacco industry. Fee projections prepared in 1996 showed that Philip Morris accounted for roughly forty percent of State Affairs's billings. State Affairs also worked for Brown & Williamson Tobacco; Covington & Burling, the tobacco industry's favorite law firm; and the National Smokers Alliance.

At Last, A Defender of the Corporate Underdog

Contributions Watch was founded in early 1996. A memo written by McCloud says the idea for the outfit "came from our work over the past two years on behalf of clients pursuing tort reform in seventeen states." Another document, an internal State Affairs business plan, said that even with the GOP's 1994 seizure of Congress, "anti-smoking activists have controlled the debate, and politicians from both parties have felt no political pain." One of the company's primary goals for its tobacco clients is to "raise the stakes for any politician who enters the fray." Most important to the firm's strategy was developing a strategy "that places a premium on actions below the radar of the anti-smoking activists. Tactics must be developed for each unique political situation and not from some standardized political play book."

This, of course, is where Contributions Watch comes in. The documents show that State Affairs provided Contributions Watch with its seed money and then recruited its executive director, Warren Miller, a former research analyst and information specialist for the Federal Election Commission. While the group's stated mission is to expose the nefarious role of money in politics, one internal memo reports that "the effect of corporate contributions is exaggerated...Most companies have an array of issues at stake in state legislatures, which dilutes the impact of their contributions on any single issue."

State Affairs exercises total control over Contributions Watch. The PR shop charges its clients for Contributions Watch's research reports and then funnels the money through to its subsidiary "watchdog." Until mid-1996, State Affairs paid Contributions Watch's employees. The watchdog then formed its own payroll but all of its employees except Warren Miller still worked out of a State Affairs office.

Having established its cover, Contributions Watch began applying for foundation grants, as well as trying to sign up corporate subscribers at $10,000 a pop. Ken Cohen, a lawyer for the Exxon Corporation, wrote a solicitation letter to big companies saying that he wanted to bring "a new 'watchdog' group" to their attention, "one which I believe deserves the business community's support." Cohen mentioned the trial lawyers' study and said that it was "of fundamental importance to legal reform efforts in the United States for this kind of data to be researched and made available to the general public." Targets of the corporate fundraising campaign included General Motors, Ford, Shell, Procter & Gamble, Mobil, Monsanto, Texaco and W.R. Grace.

Don't Forget to Lie

State Affairs knew very well that exposure of its links to Contributions Watch—particularly the tobacco connection—would be fatal. The firm's business plan says that Contributions Watch may sometimes conduct a research study for a corporate sponsor but will not release the report itself if such a step would make the mighty watchdog "look like an advocate for a particular industry." In that case, the sponsor will release the study itself, thereby serving to "inoculate CW from criticism." In a memo from 1996, Warren Miller warned that "when the trial lawyer studies currently in the pipeline are released, CW will become extremely vulnerable to attacks that we are nothing more than an arm of the tort reform industry. We need to diversify and release other studies."

Miller asked an attorney for State Affairs, Henry Hart of Hazel & Thomas, what to do if asked by reporters about the source of Contributions Watch's money. Hart suggested that Miller stonewall in cases "where you cannot preclude the possibility that the person making the inquiry has interests hostile to Contributions Watch." Based on Hart's advice, Contributions Watch devised a "Talking Points" memo to help employees deal with the press. If pressed, staffers are to admit that the trial lawyers study was "sponsored by supporters of tort reform" but to insist that Contributions Watch "is an independent, nonprofit, nonpartisan, non-ideological watchdog research and monitoring organization. We have no position on tort reform. We focus solely on the numbers."

If asked about the links between Contributions Watch and State Affairs, Miller was programmed to reply: "I worked for the FEC as an analyst, and then worked for a time at State Affairs as a research wonk. Back last year, I approached State Affairs with the idea of spinning me off as a non-profit organization. I'm happy to say that Contributions Watch is now an independent organization with our own offices and own board of directors, none of whom, I might add, are employees or directors of State Affairs."

In an adroit step designed to establish legitimacy, Contributions Watch's debut study concerned the need to strengthen state financial disclosure laws, a mom-and-apple pie topic that promised little controversy and favorable coverage. A number of newspapers, including the *Miami Herald*, the

---

August Activities Report

To: Philip Morris

Worked with reporter on comprehensive campaign finance story, initial three-hour meeting (included preparation for that meeting); day to day answering questions, meetings, developing new materials and documentation.

Ongoing coordination with APCO's, Cohn and Cooper RE: abstract information.

Ongoing coordination with APCO RE: release of other numbers.

Conference calls, 8/13; 8/20; 8/29.

New York meetings 8/14; 8/26, 8/29--with team and journalist.

Coordination with <u>Wall Street Journal</u> RE: two editorial projects.

Kennel-trained watchdog: Summary of State Affairs' work for Philip Morris. Note that the PR firm billed the tobacco giant for placing a story in the *Wall Street Journal*.

Richmond Times-Dispatch, the *Seattle Times* and the *Albuquerque Journal*, duly lauded Contributions Watch for its noble efforts.

Contributions Watch then turned to its true aim, promotion of "tort reform," with the release in July of its perversely titled report, "Off the Radar Screen: Plaintiff's Lawyer Contributions to Federal Candidates." This report was paid for with tobacco industry money, especially from Covington & Burling and Philip Morris. In August of 1996 alone, State Affairs billed the law firm for $65,547.86, much of that to cover data collection for the update. Philip Morris has even been billed by State Affairs for its work in placing the trial lawyer study in the *Wall Street Journal* and the *Weekly Standard*, as well as for time spent by PR shop staffers in "meetings with journalists in Washington to discuss story concepts." (The *Journal*'s story did report that the Contributions Watch study had received funding from "backers of tort overhaul.")

In addition to attention it has received in the media, the ersatz "watchdog" also duped some consumer groups. Mike Odom, head of the Alabama chapter of Citizen Action, was so impressed with the report on state disclosure laws that he sent a letter to Contributions Watch asking how the two organizations might work together in the future.

Before exposure of its links to tobacco destroyed the conspiracy, State Affairs was planning a Contributions Watch study that would smear Consumers Union. In a August 27 letter to Duncan MacDonald, general counsel for Citicorp, State Affairs partner Charles Francis wrote, "I think you will enjoy a major column targeting Consumers Union to appear soon on the *Wall Street Journal* editorial page. Quoting Tim McVeigh, 'Something big is going to happen'."

When You Hear the Word "Citizens,"
Reach for Your Wallet

Ask any informed citizen for the top lobby-lawyer shops in Washington and he might well mention Patton, Boggs & Blow (once home to the late Ron Brown, where he toiled energetically for such clients as "Baby Doc" Duvalier). Or Akin, Gump, Strauss, Hauer & Feld might be mentioned, home to Robert Strauss and Vernon Jordan. Our informed citizen might make a lunge at the big PR firms such as Burson-Marsteller or Hill and Knowlton. But most likely absent from the list would be Citizens for a Sound Economy (CSE)—even though it was rated by the beltway newspaper *Roll Call* in 1995 as the fourth most influential organization in Washington (after the National Federation of Independent Business, the Christian Coalition, and the National Association of Wholesaler-Distributors).

Yet *Roll Call* was on the mark. In all its 13 years, and especially during the past few, the Citizens for a Sound Economy think tank has played a decisive or significant role in virtually every major issue of national importance. A full-scale lobbying campaign by Citizens is one of the primary reasons that Bill Clinton's 1993 budget did not contain a tax on energy producers, or any significant new spending for social programs. The same can be said in explaining the defeat of health care reform in 1994. Citizens has also been perhaps the leading proponent of the conservative economic agenda, especially in regard to welfare cutbacks, "regulatory reform" and the call for lower taxes on the rich.

Making use of think tanks and front groups like CSE has become another important part of Corporate America's lobbying arsenal. These outfits not only craft the intellectual scaffolding needed to support the Fortune 500's legislative program but, as with "grassroots" efforts, provide corporations with plausible deniability as to their direct involvement in a lobbying campaign. In the 1991 report, "Masks of Deception," Mark Megalli and Andy Friedman wrote:

> [Until recently] big business corporations delivered their messages through their traditional lobbyists in Washington. The names of these old fashioned corporate lobbies told the stories—Beer Institute, National Coal Association, Chamber of Commerce, American Petroleum Institute.
>
> But as public interest groups began to win widespread public support, it became clear that new mechanisms were needed to deliver the corporate message. Thus, if Burger King were to report that a Whopper is nutritious, informed consumers would probably shrug in disbelief. If Anheuser-Busch were to report that a beer a day could lead to a happier life, consumers might see this as an another attempt to sell beer. And if the Nutrasweet company were to insist that the artificial sweetener aspartame has no side effects, consumers might not be inclined to believe them, either.
>
> But if the 'American Council on Science and Health' and its panel of 200 'expert' scientists reported that Whoppers were not so bad, consumers might actually listen. If the 'Health Education Foundation'... were to report on 'The Good of Alcohol,' beer drinkers might be less reluctant to cut down on drinking. And if the 'Calorie Control Council' reported that aspartame is not really dangerous, weight-conscious consumers might continue dumping the artificial sweetener in their coffee every morning without concern.

Incidentally, all of the groups cited above are real. The Health Education Foundation, headed by Dr. Morris Chafetz, is funded by companies such as Miller Brewing and Philip Morris, as well as United States Brewers Association and the Wine Institute. Chafetz has written numerous op-ed articles—generally being identified only as the president of the Foundation with no mention of the group's financial backers—in which he has opposed excise taxes on alcohol, derided reports that heavy drinking can cause health problems and even claimed that many drunk drivers are actually committing suicide.

Helping America Think Right

Some interesting features set Citizens apart from other big corporate-backed think tanks that now bulk so large in the political landscape of Washington. In keeping with its operating "grassroots" concept, Citizens has few stars. The American Enterprise Institute bulges with household names such as James Q. Wilson, Robert Bork and the Bellcurver himself, Charles Murray. Heritage has Richard Allen, William Bennett and Jack Kemp. Even Georgetown's blowsy Center for Strategic and International Studies can boast such second-tier "scholars" as Fred Ikle and Arnaud de Borchgrave.

Eschewing such high fliers, Citizens offers as its chairman C. Boyden Gray, White House counsel during the Bush administration and now a partner at the Washington law firm of Wilmer, Cutler & Pickering. While Gray is not an intellectual heavyweight, he has emerged as a leading bagman for the GOP. In 1995, he made more soft money contributions—$140,000, all to the Republican Party—than any other individual donor. That same year he hosted a fundraiser at his Georgetown home, with Newt Gingrich as the guest of honor, that brought in more than $1 million for the GOP. (Citizens' counselor, James Miller, was budget director under President Ronald Reagan.)

Citizens staffers are young Republicans, eager to do battle with Corporate America's foes, moving deftly across Washington's overlapping worlds of government, lobbying and policy formation. Lydia Verheggen, director of health planning, previously worked at the Heritage Foundation and, before that, the office of Sen. Paul Coverdell of Georgia. Carl Parks came to Citizens after a stint as a lobbyist for Allstate Insurance and has since become counsel at Coverdell's office.

©Shia photo/Impact Visuals

C. Boyden Gray: An advisor to George Bush and major political donor to the GOP, Gray is one of Washington's best-connected lobbyists. Chief causes: dirty air and generalized destruction of the environment, lowering taxes on the wealthy, and gutting any type of regulation of Corporate America.

Brian Lopina, formerly Citizens' director of government relations, moved on to the office of Rep. Ernest Istook of Oklahoma and after that to the Christian Coalition. Paul Merski came to Citizens from the Pharmaceutical and Research Manufacturers of America and left to join the Joint Economic Committee of Congress. Fred Nutt, a one-time staff assistant at Citizens, now works for House Speaker Newt Gingrich.

Citizens' central concern is money, not ideology. Hence, CSE steers clear of foreign policy—it never joined in the Cold War's anti-Soviet crusade and views China as an alluring market, not a threat. Instead, it focuses exclusively on economic issues. It publishes hundreds of reports and studies with predictable conclusions and equally predictable titles: *Clean Air Bill May Devastate an Already Weak Economy*, *Minimum Wage Hurts Poor* and *"Soaking the Rich" Is All Wet*.

The Darth Vader of Lobbying

What makes Citizens for a Sound Economy unique among the beltway's big think tanks is that it also runs a grassroots lobby shop. The think tank and lobbying unit are housed in the same downtown office and have overlapping staffers, funders and board members. Legally, however, they are separate enterprises, a fictitious division that allows Citizens to solicit tax-exempt contributions for its think tank and use the money to provide research and intellectual ammunition for the lobby shop (which, as an advocacy group, is barred by the Internal Revenue Service from accepting tax-deductible donations). And since Citizens does not directly lobby members of Congress or the White House but organizes "grassroots" campaigns, companies aren't required to divulge their contributions to Citizens and Citizens isn't required to reveal who pays its bills.

During its early years, Citizens relied heavily on support from a small group of right-wing foundations, most importantly three outfits controlled by David and Charles Koch, the billionaire owners of Koch Industries, the nation's largest privately owned oil company. Both Kochs are long-time conservative activists. In 1980, David Koch ran as the Libertarian Party's vice presidential candidate on a platform calling for repeal of minimum wage and child labor laws. Between 1986 and 1990, the two men funneled $4.6 million to Citizens.

Citizens won't reveal its donors but it is possible to assemble a profile of the group's finances from a combination of public and confidential sources. Among the group's biggest backers— many who have contributed tens of thousands of dollars and some hundreds of thousands of dollars—are corporations such as Amoco, Boeing, Chevron, Citicorp, CIGNA, General Electric, General Motors, Georgia-Pacific, Metropolitan Life, Mobil, Xerox, trade groups like the American Petroleum Institute and the Pharmaceutical Research and Manufacturers of America, and foundations such as John M. Olin, Sarah Scaife and Philip M. McKenna.

All conservative think tanks are supported by corporate money and produce pro-business studies and reports, but in the case of CSE, the *quid* and the *pro quo* march together in unusually tight formation. A confidential list of donors from 1991 shows that during that year Citizens took in more than $30,000 from Nissan North America, Toyota, Honda and the Coalition for Vehicle Choice, a front group for foreign importers. Before long, Citizens was leading a campaign to oppose federal tariffs on foreign minivans. The same year, Citizens received $95,000 from Bell Atlantic, NYNEX and Southwestern Bell, money used to lead a drive for the deregulation of the Baby Bells. Another of the Baby Bells, Ameritech, made donations to Citizens of $75,000 in both 1992 and 1993. In addition to its lobbying for telecommunications reform, Citizens rewarded the company with a fawning think tank report in the latter year, "The Future Is Now: Ameritech's Plan for Local Telephone Competition."

More recently, CSE has been promoting "tort reform." As always, the phrase Follow the Money provides a useful guide to Citizens' modus operandi. For among the think tank's biggest funders are the same Fortune 500 firms—insurers like Allstate, pesticide makers like Dow, chemical companies such as Union Carbide, oil companies like Exxon—that have been at the forefront of the "tort reform" movement.

Especially revealing is Citizens' rich and fragrant relationship with Philip Morris, which has made CSE one of its most favored agents. In 1991 alone, the tobacco company made three grants totaling $91,800 to Citizens' think tank and a

$100,000 lump sum contribution to the lobby shop. Further links between Citizens and the tobacco industry abound. Beverly McKittrick, formerly head of Citizens' Legal Project, joined Philip Morris's stable of Washington lobbyists. Robert Tollison, a professor at George Mason University and board member of the Citizens think tank, serves as a consultant to the tobacco industry. R.J. Reynolds, the nation's second largest tobacco company, also donates to Citizens, though in amounts which remain secret. "We were quite pleased with their work," Craig Fuller, a former top aide to George Bush and lobbyist for Philip Morris, told *National Journal.* "Because of their willingness to take on certain issues publicly and frontally, they're able to get support from businesses and business associations." Another lobbyist, John Motley of the National Retail Federation, admitted to the *Journal* that CSE basically serves as a money laundering operation for Corporate America. "They take major companies who want to get something accomplished but are not willing to have their names out front," he said.

My Life as a Bagman, Part II

I gained special access to Citizens by making a contribution of $100, which elicited a flood of promotional material and invitations to membership events which are closed to the public. My first up close look came on a blustery winter evening in 1996, when some 60 people gathered at CSE's headquarters in downtown Washington to attend its "Campaign Kickoff." The event was intended to rally the troops for upcoming legislative battles, introduce a few new Citizens staffers to the organization's corporate patrons and, of course, encourage the latter to unbuckle a few more dollars.

Though the word bulks so large in the group's agitprop, "grassroots" did not entirely evoke the atmosphere. Other than a dozen or so of Citizens twenty- and thirty-something policy technicians, and me, the Kickoff crowd was composed almost entirely of lobbyists and special interest groups, the very forces of darkness that Citizens professes to oppose.

The heavy armor that evening took the form of plenipotentiaries from the cream of the Fortune 500. There was Tim Hyde, a public relations man from R.J. Reynolds' Winston-Salem corporate office; Richard Kimberly, head of federal government relations at Kimberly Clark, the Dallas-based paper company; Walt Buchholtz from Exxon Chemical Company's Houston offices; Dr. Jane Work, a vice president at the National Association of Manufacturers; Patrick Gaston, a lobbyist with NYNEX; Ken Yale, a senior vice president at the Jefferson Group, a big corporate consulting firm; as well as representatives from Fortune 500 companies like Philip Morris, Intel, Bell Atlantic and Edison Electric. The light infantry consisted of fraternal delegates from assorted conservative think tanks—Laura Peterson of the Hoover Institution and Bruce Bartlett of the National Center for Policy Alternatives—and a few GOP congressional staffers, including J.T. Young, an economist for the Senate Republican Policy Committee.

Citizens occupies much of the seventh floor of its building but the Kickoff audience arranged itself in the sparsely decorated front room. They gathered in groups of twos and threes, huddling near the open bar and generously stocked banquet table, overflowing with demure steak sandwiches, curry chicken skewers, cold shrimp, fresh fruits and pastries. There was plenty of uniformed help on hand, holding aloft platters from which people replenished their empty plates.

Citizens staffers engaged guests in earnest conversations about utility deregulation, telecommunications reform and the political economy of digital television. One invitee, holding an empty drink and anxious to return to the bar, swiveled his eyes nervously, clearly eager to escape from a Citizens telecommunications specialist giving a prolonged sermon on the manner in which liberals have "exploited concerns about universal service" in seeking to slow deregulation of the industry.

After an hour of hors d'oeuvres and cocktails, Paul Beckner, Citizens' president, rose to pronounce the official welcome. Beckner praised Congress for having passed the telecommunications reform bill, a measure long sought by Citizens and by a number of the corporate representatives on hand. He noted with pleasure that Steve Forbes—then briefly riding high in polls for the Republican presidential nomination—had done much to popularize the "flat tax," another of Citizens' most cherished goals.

Adopting a graver tone, Beckner pointed toward the audience and noted the presence of Leah Geraghty, coordinator of the Citizens Roundtable, a program designed to conjure subventions of $25,000 and up from the donors. "Some of you might be hearing from Leah by the end of the month," Beckner remarked.

"By the end of the night!," Geraghty merrily cried.

Beckner then introduced Nancy Mitchell, a refugee from Dan Quayle's Council on Competitiveness and now a Citizens vice president. Mitchell quickly moved through a laundry list of the group's priorities: less government regulation, free trade, overhauling of the legal system, a balanced budget. The key to achieving the latter, said Mitchell, is "cutting spending, not raising taxes. We can't do it unless we're willing to take on the 800-pound gorilla called entitlements." The audience, roused at the mention of juicy targets like Social Security, Medicare and welfare, murmured in approval.

Despite their total dominance of American political life, conservatives never tire of insisting that national institutions—the press, the universities, the public schools—are controlled by leftist infiltrators. Surrounded by some of America's premier corporate donors, Mitchell decried the strength of Citizens' adversaries, especially environmentalists. "The Sierra

Club has succeeded in getting its handbooks into the kinder-gartens," she said, indicating that this tactical master stroke alone had placed Citizens and its allies at an extreme disad-vantage in the war of ideas.

The complaints against the enviro crowd were as nothing against the scorn and abuse heaped on then Food and Drug Administration Commissioner David Kessler, dubbed by Mitchell as the man "we all love to hate." Appointed by George Bush and shepherded through the nomination process by Utah Senator Orrin Hatch, Kessler is an unlikely enemy of the right. But he earned the enmity of industry by seeking to revive an agency that for most of the past decade has been moribund. Worse still for Citizens' friends in the tobacco industry, he labeled nicotine a drug that should be subject to regulation.

After brief remarks from several other Citizens staffers, the audience returned to the task of finishing off the food and drink. During a relentless, multi-pronged assault on the buffet table, John Berlau of Consumer Alert—a Citizens ally founded by John Sununu, George Bush's chief of staff—derided Ralph Nader and mandatory air bags in automobiles with equal vigor. "People shouldn't be forced to buy air bags," Berlau exclaimed, offering up his vision of consumer activism, "They're an added cost that shouldn't be mandatory."

With a snow storm expected, many guests soon began to straggle out. Berlau, though, was just getting warmed up. After I begged off, he turned his attention to a man sifting through the buffet table's dwindling supply of pastries and launched into a fresh denunciation of Nader's malign influence on the body politic.

Organizing the Elite:
  Making the World Safe for the Kochs

With Citizens' growing prestige of recent years has come a great deal more money. By 1994, its budget had topped $10 million and in 1996 it leapt to more than $17 million, putting it in the same league as long established think tanks like the American Enterprise Institute and the Cato Institute.

Brent Bahler, a Citizens spokesman, makes much of the $15 and $20 checks that come in from Citizens' 250,000 members, who are mostly recruited via direct mail. He says that "small" donors—defined quite broadly as those giving $1,000 or less—provide the group with a significant share of its funding. But foundations run by the Koch family are still the single largest donor to Citizens, kicking in nearly $750,000 in 1994 and more than $1 million in 1993.

The links between the Koch family and Citizens extend far beyond the realm of finance. David Koch sits on the Citizens' board. So, too, does Richard Fink, who attended UCLA and NYU graduate school on Koch scholarships and later became Koch Industries' registered lobbyist in Washington. Gracing the board of Citizens' lobby shop is Wayne Gable, another one-time Koch lobbyist and now head of the Center for Market Processes, a Koch-funded department at George Mason University in Fairfax, Virginia.

There exists a remarkable confluence of interests between Citizens and the Kochs on the political front as well. In 1993, Bill Clinton's budget plan included a $72 billion energy tax, a proposal viewed with dread and loathing by Koch and other oil companies. Between April and May of that year, Citizens received donations from Chevron, Mobil, and El Paso Natural Gas. This coincided with a highly prolific period at the think tank, which coughed up at least six reports on the so-called BTU tax, demonstrating that it would cripple the trucking industry, burden farmers, send gasoline prices soaring, injure the family and ravage the state of Virginia.

To mobilize the citizenry, Citizens sent a direct mail packet to some 16,000 "grass-tops" leaders—business and community leaders thought to have special clout with elected officials—who were urged to write anti-BTU letters to their senators and to President Clinton, and mail them back to Washington in an enclosed prepaid express mail package. Recipients of the packet were then contacted by a telemarketing firm that offered to patch through a call to Congress at no expense to the grassroots protester. In some states, Citizens also held festive outdoor rallies as part of its campaign. The offer of a free lunch, including chocolate cake, helped draw a crowd of hundreds to Billings, Montana.

Citizens also worked in conjunction with the American Energy Alliance, which coordinated opposition to the BTU tax in Oklahoma, Montana, Louisiana and other battleground states. Within a month of its founding in May of 1993, the alliance had spent more than $2 million and hired 120 lobbyists, whose efforts were coordinated by Jim McAvoy of the Burson-Marsteller public relations firm.

Paul Beckner, Citizens' Napoleon of the grassroots, kept Koch Industries intimately aware of his outfit's efforts to kill the BTU tax. On May 6, he sent Richard Fink, then a Koch lobbyist, a memorandum saying that "the cornerstone of CSE's strategy to stop the Clinton tax plan" was to kill the BTU in the Senate Finance Committee, where "we need only two votes" (the Committee at the time had eleven Democrats and nine Republicans). On May 26, he faxed an "update on the BTU Tax Project" to three Koch Industry executives in which he summarized Citizens' direct mail and telephone campaigns and included a few "letters to members of Congress our efforts are producing."

The campaign worked to perfection. Democratic Senators John Breaux of Louisiana and David Boren of Oklahoma, both who had been targeted by CSE and the Alliance, came out against Clinton, forcing him to strike the energy tax before the Finance Committee would approve his budget.

In mounting a campaign, Citizens first identifies members of Congress who are wavering on a given piece of legislation. Then, field operatives—often GOP political leaders or Republican consultants—are hired in the states or districts represented by these potential swing voters. To develop and refine its message, particularly to appeal to stubbornly resistant groups, Citizens will sometimes assemble "focus groups." Spokesman Bahler told me that one session held in Buffalo, New York, in preparation of Citizens' work on the GATT treaty, revealed that workers who'd been hard hit by foreign imports and who are normally hostile to free trade, respond well to a message exalting the high quality of American-made goods and pride in the nation's ability to compete with its international competitors. Next comes a media campaign with radio and television ads used to generate mail, telegrams and phone calls to targeted members of Congress. All of this takes place with assistance from hired guns plucked from the capital's swollen ranks of corporate lobbyists and PR flacks.

The public face of Citizens' campaigns is invariably a "broad-based" coalition listing hundreds of members but discreetly funded and controlled by a few big interests. These coalitions rise with a given piece of legislation and fold when their mission has been accomplished. To press for trucking deregulation, Citizens worked with the hastily concocted Transportation Reform Alliance; to push for tax cuts there was the evanescent Coalition for Fiscal Restraint; to reduce funding for Medicare there's the brazenly named Coalition to Save Medicare; to lobby for a balanced budget there's the worthy Coalition for America's Future.

In 1994, Citizens mounted a major operation to kill the Clinton administration's health care plan. Coordinating Citizens' drive was Elizabeth Sauer, whom the lobby shop hired away from the Fleishman-Hillard public relations firm and bedecked with the impressive title of "Director of Mobilization." Citizens drew up plans for a "Middle Class Truth Squad" to lead the campaign, which was funded by its big donors (at least one contributor was the Olin Foundation, which ponied up $25,000).

A funding proposal for the "truth squad" campaign offers a good idea of what the group means by "grassroots" organizing. Out of a budget set at $321,000, Citizens allocated $42,000 to shuttle its staffers around the country to distribute baseball caps, Frisbees and buttons. Another $8,000 was budgeted for counter-rallies in towns to be visited by the Clintonites' "Health Security Express" bus tour, with Citizens staffers on hand to greet the administration's troops with a towed bus called the "Phony Express."

The vast majority of the money—$266,000—was slotted to pay for a media campaign that painted Clinton's plan as the first step on the path toward "government-run health care," a Soviet-style nightmare in which everyone would "pay more for less care." One TV ad contained the following exchange:

Man: Gatekeeper!
Woman: Hello? This is Mrs. Taylor. My son is having a terrible earache and needs to see Dr. Murray right away."
Man: You will not see Dr. Murray. Dr. Johnson will see your son next week!"
Woman: Next week? He needs a doctor now! Is Dr. Johnson an ear specialist?
Man: It doesn't matter.

Such ads saturated local markets in the days leading up to the arrival of the Health Security Express and helped draw big crowds to CSE's rallies. The humiliating PR debacle suffered by Clinton's forces foreshadowed the defeat of the administration's health care bill in Congress and the amputation of the topic from public debate for two years.

Fouling the Air: Citizens Takes on the Mormons

A more recent target of CSE has been clean air, more specifically tighter rules on pollution proposed by the Environmental Protection Agency in 1996. Nearly 200 scientific studies have shown that our air is more and more toxic. Each year, 60,000 Americans die prematurely due to respiratory ailments and heart attacks linked to fine particle exposure. Respiratory problems are now the No. 1 cause of hospital admissions for children.

Much of these illnesses are caused by industrial pollution. The EPA rules so feared by CSE were proposed after a study found that when a Geneva Steel Co. plant in Provo, Utah was running full tilt, hospital admissions for lung ailments shot up dramatically. For children, they doubled. The conclusions of the study, which examined the 1986 to 1987 period, were virtually impossible to dispute. Much of Provo's population is Mormons, who don't smoke, and there is no other industry in the area. Tiny particles from the steel plant were the only possible culprit.

Needless to say, the EPA's proposed tightening of clean air standards threw industry into a panic. A front group called the Air Quality Standards Coalition soon formed, its members including the National Association of Manufacturers (NAM), Geneva Steel, Texaco, Philip Morris, Chevron, Monsanto and the American Petroleum Institute. First, coalition members tried to discredit the Provo report's science. Gerald Esper of the Automobile Manufacturers said the study's findings were exaggerated because "many of the deaths are of elderly people and others who are sick and who would have died anyway." The American Iron and Steel Institute commissioned a study to show that the cost of complying with the EPA rules would be staggeringly high. As it turned out, the study actually showed that there would be no cost involved. "So let's deep-six [it]," one member of the coalition said during a meeting, according to a transcript obtained by *The New Republic*. "Won't see the light of day."

Faced with such obstacles, the coalition turned for help to CSE, a natural choice since among Chairman Gray's clients at his law firm is Geneva Steel. CSE swiftly launched a multi-million dollar "educational" campaign against the EPA rules, much of it financed by members of the coalition (the American Petroleum Institute alone agreed to match all donations up to $600,000). CSE claimed that its campaign was based on an opinion survey it conducted but in fact its program was completely contrary to the opinions it found. "Most Americans (76 percent) consider themselves to be 'environmentalists,'" reads the survey introduction, according to *The New Republic*. "Few voters say they know someone who has been adversely affected by EPA laws or regulations, while a larger number say they know someone whose health has been negatively affected by a poor environment." The poll report went on to say that CSE staff should work hard to convince voters that they are pro-environment: "You have children, you are an outdoor photographer or sportsman, you enjoy the beauty of our natural resources."

In the end, President Clinton issued air pollution standards that he called "very strong." In fact, the president, as he normally does when confronted with the forces of darkness, had caved. Hidden between the lines were a number of provisions that surely warmed the hearts of the CSE crowd. Cities won't need to submit plans to meet the new standards until 2002, and won't have to meet the standards for at least another decade thereafter. The White House scaled back its original proposal on ozone by 20 percent. Clinton ordered the EPA to go easy on Eastern states that have taken steps to reduce acid rain. The end result of these compromises is that thousands of Americans will continue to die each year from breathing toxic air.

Losing Sleep Over the FDA

Few targets have ranked higher on the corporate agenda these past few years than the Food and Drug Administration. Providing the ideological firepower for the campaign are CSE and a number of other beltway think tanks—the Hudson Institute, Newt Gingrich's Progress and Freedom Foundation, the Cato Institute, among others—which claim that FDA dawdling has resulted in the untimely demise of tens of thousands of U.S. citizens and that the private sector could provide review faster and more efficiently than government bureaucrats.

CSE has spent millions on its anti-FDA effort, which has included newspaper and radio advertising campaigns and the publication of countless reports charging the FDA with incompetence and misconduct. CSE's campaign has not been without its humorous elements. In 1995, Chairman Gray told members of a House subcommittee of one particularly egregious example of FDA dallying, the case of the miracle drug nitrazepam. The drug "was approved five years later in the United States than it was in Britain," Gray thundered. "In that five year period...more than 3,700 Americans could have been saved." The force of Gray's presentation was greatly diminished when Rep. Richard Durbin informed CSE's leader that the "life-saving" drug nitrazepam is used to treat insomnia, an unpleasant though not normally fatal ailment.

Most of the charges leveled against the FDA by CSE and other think tanks are bogus. The FDA has already dramatically reduced approval times for new drug applications, from an average of 33 months in 1987 to 16.5 months in 1996. For drugs that were deemed to constitute major therapeutic advances, the review time was just six months. And, most tellingly, during recent years, the FDA has kept off the U.S. market 47 drugs which had been approved for sale in England, France and Germany, and which were all later withdrawn in those countries due to safety problems.

Though CSE claims the FDA is too nitpicky in its oversight role, many dangerous drugs still find their way to pharmacy shelves. Thomas Moore, a senior fellow at George Washington University's Center for Health Policy research, says prescription drugs annually injure about 5 million U.S. citizens seriously enough to require medical treatment. Moore says deaths could be 100,000 or more and estimates that you are 10 times more likely to be severely injured by a prescribed drug than in a car accident.

Organizing the Grasstops

But the campaign against the FDA has nothing to do with protecting the public and everything to do with helping corporations speed their drugs to market with minimal scrutiny from government health officials. This point was starkly illustrated the last time I saw Citizens close up, at an all-day affair it held in May of 1996 at the J.W. Marriott on Pennsylvania Avenue, under the chipper title, "The American Economy: Opportunities for Positive Change." The "A" list was out in force. There were at least three representatives from Koch Industries, including David Koch. There were officials from CIGNA, Dow Chemical, Texaco, Domino's Pizza, Northrop Grumman, Columbia Gas, the U.S. Chamber of Commerce and the National Association of Manufacturers. There were delegations from think tanks such as Cato and the Washington Legal Foundation, as well as "grassroots" activists from the Seniors Coalition and United Seniors, two groups working with Citizens to gut Medicare. Finally, there were dozens of individual Citizens donors on hand, mingling excitedly with the beltway elite.

Rep. Joe Scarborough of Florida, one of the more rabid GOP freshmen swept in to office in 1994, drew cheers from the crowd when he called for the elimination of the Departments of Energy, Commerce, Education and Housing and Urban Development. In discussing political strategy,

Scarborough drew spacious historical parallels, saying that the GOP's mistake had been to hesitate, here invoking Hannibal, who terrorized the Roman Empire for 17 years but hesitated to attack Rome itself. Only if Rome fell, would the empire fall. By the time he did attack, the Romans were ready and defeated him. Fast forward to 1995: when controversy erupted over GOP's plan to cut school lunches, Republicans, said Scarborough, should have stood up and said, "You're darn right, we not only favor cutting lunches administered by the federal government, we want to abolish [the program].... We have to charge ahead, we can't hesitate like Hannibal." Scarborough also lamented the fact that from a PR perspective, the Republicans will always lose. "There's always gonna be a 5-year-old African-American in the South Bronx who can be tied to spending cuts" and those cuts will then be "blamed on Republican sons of bitches."

Both invited panelists and Citizens staffers took pains to stress how refreshing it was to be in a room full of down-to-earth folk from "outside the beltway." Indeed, many "real" Americans—albeit mostly millionaires—were assembled at the Marriott. Every so often someone in the crowd would inadvertently bring attention to the unusual character of this gathering of grassroots activists. During a question-and-answer period, Nancy Centofante, a doctor from Maryland and member of the Citizens President's Council ($1,000 and up donors), strode to the microphone and argued that conservatives needed to be less "geeky" in seeking to communicate with the public. "Most of us in this room are employers," she said forthrightly. "We need to reach employees." The message that needs to be conveyed, Centofante continued, is that in their zeal to "soak the rich," workers are forcing CEOs to shift their companies' operations abroad, where labor is cheaper and more docile.

This was no "ideas" conference, though, but an event designed to impress donors with Citizens' importance. Trophy congressmen—in addition to Scarborough there were Senators James Inhofe of Oklahoma, Larry Craig of Idaho and Don Nickles of Oklahoma, and House Whip Richard Armey—were prominently on display, as were GOP political consultants. Many donors excitedly lined up for a photo-op with the perennially grinning Steve Forbes, the keynote speaker for the affair's dinner.

The hoped -for transfer of wealth was carefully scripted, as seen in a confidential memo to Citizens staffers. At the conference lunch, held at the National Press Club, there would be, the memo confided, nine tables of ten people, with two seats reserved at each for staffers, one a policy specialist and the other a grassroots practitioner. This would allow the donors to get a full sweep of the Citizens menu: "As table host, you will carry the conversation through lunch after Nancy [Mitchell] and Walter [Williams, Citizens board member] have finished making remarks. Your role will be to sell CSE to the donors at your table...If you see donors you know, especially ones who are interested in your issue, encourage them to sit at your table, or follow them to their table and use the opportunity to sell the donors on CSE's most recent activities."

Before the dinner, people mingled and schmoozed over cocktails from an open bar. Ed Crane of the Cato Institute exchanged fundraising tips with colleagues, complaining about one Chicago donor who'd "sent in a check for $10,000, wrote me a letter saying he was happy to share the universe with me, and then disappeared!"

A vibrant Centofante milled about, expressing excitement and astonishment upon learning that another doctor was at the affair. "I've never met another physician at [a CSE event]," she exclaimed. "The people I meet all own their own factory or something." Justin Keller from Tennessee is another happy Citizens donor. He has attended classes at the Virginia-based Leadership Institute, an outfit which trains conservatives to run for public office. Like Centofante, Keller worries about the difficulty of communicating with "Joe Six-Pack" and said he was going to "camp out at Wal-Mart" to pick up pointers. Fortunately, said Keller, "My second language is redneck."

Sugar Daddy

But this was also a day where donors could cash in their chips. Curbing the power of the FDA was a top priority for a number of pharmaceutical companies and medical device manufacturers who were represented at the conference. Terry Adkins, a representative of Pittsburgh-based Biocontrol Technology Inc., huddled with Citizens' government relations assistant, Jenny Rugland, and complained about an FDA panel's unanimous decision in late February to keep his company's Diasensor 1000 off the market until further tests are conducted. The Diasensor, which allows diabetics to use infrared light to measure blood sugar levels instead of drawing blood, is of huge import to Biocontrol, which has invested more than $65 million developing the device. On the day that the FDA rejected its use, the company's stock tumbled by 41 percent.

The problem for the company is that during testing the Diasensor measured blood sugar accurately in only 8 of 23 cases. Even the Juvenile Diabetes Foundation has opposed approval of the device, because erroneous information about a patient's blood sugar level can be fatal.

After a lengthy discussion, during which Rugland talked about FDA reform bills Citizens is trying to get through Congress, she offered to introduce Adkins to James Prendergrast, Citizens new Mobilization Director. "That's one of the reasons I came down," Adkins said gratefully. And perhaps here—with a businessman trying to shove his defective contraption past the government's watchdogs—is where we should take our leave of this grassroots assembly of good citizens, as they eagerly awaited Steve Forbes, prophet of that great leveler of wealth, the flat tax.

CHAPTER FOUR

FOREIGN LOBBYING

Voices of the Damned

"Agents of influence are generally of two types, unwitting and witting. Unwitting agents are rare. They can be given the benefit of the doubt. Much more common are those who are motivated by monetary gain. They are people who are prepared to place Chinese interests ahead of their own country's for money."

—Peter Lund, Senior China analyst for Canadian intelligence

There is a baneful climate surrounding the world of domestic lobbying, with business's hired guns seeking to fatten corporate welfare programs at the expense of waifs and orphans. When it comes to foreign lobbying, the atmosphere becomes positively toxic. Here, Washington's finest work to enhance the image of Third World despots guilty of mass murder, corruption and other assorted crimes against humanity.

Foreign lobbying is an especially lucrative field as First World economic competitors and Third World regimes shell out enormous sums of money in the hopes that a well-coordinated campaign will win them favorable media coverage and friends in Congress. Both of these commodities are essential to the ultimate goals of heading off trade sanctions or generating copious flows of American financial aid. Foreign governments spent $86 million to lobby the U.S. government during the first six months of 1996, according to *The Hill* newspaper. The money was paid to 2,825 lobbyists representing 595 firms.

Japan was the biggest spender, unbuckling $17.8 million, far more than the $8.7 million ponied up by the Bahamas. Other countries in the top ten were Mexico, Hong Kong and India.

What's ironic is that foreign regimes generally get little bang for their bucks. Dictators seem to overestimate the benefits that can be reaped by retaining a D.C. influence peddler, perhaps because the highly effective "lobbying" tools they employ at home—bombing opposition newspapers to ensure favorable coverage, murdering political opponents to ensure rubber stamp support from elected bodies—are frowned upon in Washington, where money and political influence can achieve the same ends more quietly.

Hitler's Little Helper

Foreign lobbying has always been the sleaziest realm of the influence peddling trade. Back in 1933, the public relations pioneer Ivy Lee was hired by the German industrial giant I.G. Farben—which later manufactured Zyklon-B for use in gas chambers—to help put a warm, cuddly face on Hitler's Nazi government. Lee's firm, which received a $25,000 per year contract, produced a report suggesting that Joachim von Ribbentrop, Hitler's foreign minister, should "undertake a definite campaign to clarify the American mind" via newspaper op-eds and radio addresses to the U.S. public.

Flacking for fascists remains a popular Washington pastime. Any dictator, no matter how vile, can easily hire himself a lobbyist to represent his interests in Washington. Big firms such as Black, Manafort, Stone and Kelly shilled for Mobutu Sese Seko, the murderous Zairian despot who robbed his country of an estimated $5 billion before being forced from power in 1997. Indonesia's Suharto, who took charge of his nation following a 1965 coup in which 1 million people were killed, has retained a steady stream of American spinmeisters to touch up his image. Feeding from the Indonesia trough are firms such as Burson-Marsteller, White & Case, and Crowell and Moring

International. Not even the whales have escaped the wrath of beltway lobbyists. The powerhouse firm of Akin, Gump signed a deal with Norway to help convince the American public and Congress that Oslo's skippers should be allowed to hunt the world's dwindling whale population, even though almost every other country has agreed to halt the practice.

The cut-throat nature of foreign lobbying has worsened in recent years, as Congress has cut back on foreign assistance programs to America's former allies in the holy war against Communism. In the late-1980s, a beltway lobbyist named Dennis Neill represented Pakistan's dictator, Zia ul-Haq. Unfortunately for Neill, Zia was dispatched by a plane bomb. Elections were held and the winner, Benazir Bhutto, replaced Neill with a PR firm headed by Mark Siegel, a Carter administration veteran. But Neill refused to relinquish the lucrative account, ceding only when Bhutto sent him a personal letter informing him that his services were no longer desired. Soon an anonymous letter—later traced to Neill, according to a lobbyist familiar with the case—that remarked unfavorably upon Siegel's religious affiliation was sent to the rabidly anti-Semitic Pakistani press, which soon began referring to Bhutto's rep as "the big Jew."

Putting The Spin on Child Labor

With many Third World dictators strapped for cash, lobbyists, like those attorneys who troll emergency rooms and traffic courts, must now aggressively court new business. Consider a pitch that Tony Smith of Schmeltzer, Aptaker & Shepard sent to an official at the embassy of the Philippines in Washington. Dated September 13, 1996, just ten days after the U.S. Department of Labor revealed plans to investigate the use of child labor in the Philippines, Smith proposed that his firm be hired to help explain away the Philippines' dismal treatment of workers and use of child labor.

Smith's letter drips with insincerity. He ingratiatingly stated that he was "surprised to hear" that the Philippines was to be investigated for its use of child labor—as if Smith, who before moving to Washington in early 1996 served as the state of Alaska's commissioner of commerce, had even the vaguest notion about the incidence of child labor in that country. If he did, Smith wouldn't have been surprised at all. The government in Manila acknowledges that 3.7 million Philippine children work, including 2 million in hazardous conditions. Kids sew, trim and embroider at garment sweatshops; weed, cut cane and apply fertilizers at sugar plantations; and assemble pieces, weave seats and varnish wood in the rattan furniture sector. They work up to eleven hours per day, get paid less than the minimum wage and sometimes receive only food in exchange for their labor. But while the words "child labor" provoke moral outrage in most, Smith's response is merely Pavlovian: a potential client is in trouble; the scent of money hangs in the air.

With equal parts candor and oil, Smith makes his case. The issue of child labor is a "major issue for the Clinton administration," he writes, which roughly translated means: "You've got a problem that requires my services." Smith knows that few issues provoke a stronger sense of revulsion among the American consumer than the use of child and sweatshop labor, which puts the Philippines in a delicate situation. The U.S. provides the country with nearly $50 million per year in economic aid, a fraction of what was lavished on Manila during the Cold War but still making it the third largest recipient in Asia behind India and Indonesia. The U.S. also buys more than $2 billion worth of Filipino goods annually, more than one-third of the country's total exports. Most relevant here, as a developing nation, the Philippines receives special trade privileges that allow its exports to enter the U.S. tariff-free— yet these privileges depend on the recipient nation offering "internationally recognized rights" to workers, including a ban

on child labor. Indeed, on the day that Smith penned his solic-
itation, the office of the U.S. Trade Representative was still
reviewing whether to strip the Philippines' special trade status
due precisely to the growing incidence of child labor in the
country, as well as officially sanctioned anti-union activities in
government-run export zones.

In seeking to reel in his catch, Smith casually dropped the
names of his beltway connections. In his letter, he mentions
his supposedly ready access to Gare Smith, the man in charge
of child labor issues at the State Department, whose efforts
Tony Smith pledges to "redirect." Smith also describes his
"excellent relationship" at the AFL-CIO, which he will seek to
"neutralize" on his client's behalf. But Smith greatly inflated
his standing with beltway power brokers in order to impress his
would-be client. The totality of his relationship with the AFL-
CIO seems to consist of modest financial support the labor federation offered to Smith for his 1992 and 1994 campaigns for
public office, both of which ended when Alaskan voters rejected his candidacy. When asked to comment about the alleged
fraternal ties between Smith and the AFL-CIO, a federation
official said, "Smith doesn't have close ties here. In fact, he has
no relationship at all."

Alas, despite Smith's pleading, the Philippines ultimately
chose not to retain his firm, perhaps because the impoverished
country was already feeling stretched a bit thin. At the time
that Smith made his pitch, the Philippines already had contracts with eleven lobby shops, who were paid at least $1 mil-
lion in 1996 to do everything from touch up the country's
human rights record to seek a greater U.S. market share for the
Philippine's exports of sugar and textiles. It is likely that an
equally powerful blow to Smith's chances came in early
October, just weeks after the lobbyist sent off his letter to the
embassy. The U.S. Trade Rep then decided that it would give
the Philippines more time to improve its record on child labor

and renewed the country's trade privileges.

Don't feel too bad for Smith, though. There are plenty of other global PR challenges waiting to be tackled. In Asia alone there's China (prison labor), Burma (slave labor) and Thailand (child prostitutes). And even though his pitch to the Philippines was rebuffed, there are an estimated 250 million kids at work around the globe, from Kenya to Brazil to India. Smith, no doubt, swiftly returned to the chase.

This is the Tale of Our Castaways...

For foreign nations facing PR difficulties in the U.S., few tactics promise more certain results than offering expense-paid junkets to Washington opinion-makers. Not many people covet trips to Saudi Arabia or Iceland, of course, but governments that can provide sandy beaches or spectacular scenery have an excellent chance of winning friends in Washington by offering free visits to their nations.

The Commonwealth of the Northern Mariana Islands (CNMI), a U.S. territory in the Pacific, has been a highly popular junket destination during the past few years. In addition to members of Congress and staffers, the administration of CNMI Governor Froilan Tenorio (who left office in early 1998) has flown squadrons of conservative journalists and think tankers to the Marianas. The goal is to fend off a move in Congress—led by Senator Daniel Akaka and Representative George Miller, and backed by the Clinton administration—that would make the CNMI subject to U.S. minimum wage and immigration law.

The effort seems to be working. Numerous junketeers have come back singing the praises of the CNMI, from the floor of Congress to newspapers such as the *Washington Times* and the *Wall Street Journal*. The legislation remains bottled up on the Hill, and House leaders vow it will never be voted on.

Located almost 4,000 miles from Hawaii, the CNMI entered into a covenant with the U.S in 1986 that gives U.S.

Marianas: Temperatures hover in the 80s year-round in the Commonwealth of the Northern Marianas, making it a favorite stop for congressional junketeers. In addition to sailing, junketeers are forced to endure a cruel regime of golf, snorkeling and tanning by hotel pools.

citizenship and local self-government to its people but, unlike all other U.S. territories, allows the Marianas government to set a local minimum wage. Only CNMI and American Samoa control their own immigration policy. (I've included the CNMI story in this chapter on foreign lobbying because it is a territory, not a state, and because the junket strategy is typically favored by foreign regimes.)

The situation has been a boon for local businesses, especially the $500-million-a-year garment industry. It relies overwhelmingly on foreign workers, mostly Chinese and Filipino, who are paid about $3 per hour. Employees are forced to work long hours and many are housed in run-down industrial barracks. "Leading members of the CNMI government assert that the Commonwealth's immigration and minimum wage laws are responsible for its economic progress," concludes a report by Democratic staffers at the House Resources Committee. "Upon closer examination, it is evident that the economic growth of the CNMI is largely due to federal grants totaling hundreds of millions of dollars and the financial success of a few employers who have relied upon the recruitment and sweat of a large, cheap, foreign labor force."

The CNMI's junket campaign is being coordinated by the D.C. offices of Preston, Gates, Ellis & Rouvelas Meeds, which Tenorio's government retained in 1996 and has since paid more than $2 million. Between April of 1996 and December of 1997, Preston, Gates arranged for six House members to visit the CNMI. Representatives Ralph Hall, Brian Bilbray and John Duncan brought their wives along on the fact-finding mission, while Representative Dana Rohrabacher of California was accompanied by his fiancée.

More than 70 congressional staffers or party officials, mostly Republicans, have also trekked to the Marianas at the expense of the CNMI government. Five staffers from Majority Leader Dick Armey's office have made the journey to the Pacific, as have employees of House Speaker Newt Gingrich, House Whip Tom DeLay and Representative Don Young of Alaska, who chairs the committee with oversight of the CNMI.

Conservative reporters and think tankers have also flocked to the Marianas. Three editorial staffers for the *Washington Times* have made the expense-paid pilgrimage to the CNMI. So, too have journalists with publications such as *Public Interest* and *National Interest*, as well as representatives from a long list of think tanks that includes the Cato Institute, the Institute for Justice, the Competitive Enterprise Institute, the Heritage Foundation, Citizens for a Sound Economy and Citizens Against Government Waste.

Preston, Gates arranges for the junketeers to stay at the

Hyatt Regency on the main island of Saipan, where prices for a single room range from $240 to $370. The Hyatt Regency, according to the hotel brochure, "lies on 14 acres of lush, tropical gardens, lagoons and magnificent micro beach...All 325 rooms have balconies and an ocean view...the exclusive Regency Club pool is framed by tropical gardens and a relaxing sun-deck. Complimentary use of the Club Elan Fitness Center, including the health club, steam room, sauna, and spa area is included in the room rate." Most junketeers go for a period of about five days with the cost of transportation, food and lodging running at almost $6,000 a head.

A sample itinerary reveals that between meals, junketeers are mostly chaperoned by local government officials and businessmen. They visit garment factories run by Willie Tan, a naturalized U.S. citizen and widely considered to be CNMI's most powerful business leader. In 1992, Tan was fined $9 million by the Labor Department for violations of U.S. labor and safety laws.

Jason Bertsch took a trip to the CNMI in early 1997 March when he was managing editor of *Public Interest*. Now at Bill Bennett's Empower America, Bertsch told me that junketeers attend a fair number of informational meetings but said there was "plenty of time" for fact-finding missions to the beach and local golf courses. He conceded that it was "problematic" for journalists to accept such trips and said tour organizers tried to put the best spin on the situation in the Marianas: "I took a moped ride around Saipan and saw workers' barracks that were pretty bad. It looked like public housing in D.C. They didn't show us that side of the island."

Governor Tenorio appears be getting a good return on his investment. In June of 1997, Representatives Armey and DeLay wrote CNMI's leader to congratulate him on "advancing the principles of free markets." They also assured him that "this Congress has no intention of voting on" reform legislation affecting the CNMI. In September, junketeer Rohrabacher took to the House floor to champion the CNMI, saying, "They have had a great deal of reform, free enterprise reform, in the last five years that has totally turned around their economy." The following month, Rohrabacher, Bilbray and Duncan hosted a luncheon for Tenorio when CNMI's governor visited Washington.

Journalism is a Beach

Junketeering journalists and think tankers have been equally helpful. Helle Bering-Jensen, deputy editorial page editor of the *Washington Times*, traveled to the CNMI in March of 1997 and wrote an enthusiastic op-ed about Tenorio's administration a month later. David Dickson, an editorial writer for the *Times*, departed on a junket in late May of 1997. A week after returning, he wrote an unsigned editorial saying that forcing the CNMI to pay workers the minimum wage "would jeopardize the economic livelihood" of the islands' people. Neither acknowledged that the CNMI had spent thousands of dollars to fly them to the Pacific.

Bering-Jensen told me that the *Times* doesn't have a policy prohibiting junkets and that she had no qualms about making the journey. "We're an editorial page," she said. "We get lobbied all the time." Dickson said that he spoke to CNMI critics before writing the editorial and that the junket had not influenced his personal views.

As for the think tanks, spokeswoman Emily McGee of the Competitive Enterprise Institute told me it was impossible that anyone there had gone, saying proudly, "We accept no government money." It turns out that Marlo Lewis, CEI's executive director, did in fact visit the Marianas in mid-1996.

Julian Weiss, a spokesman at the Heritage Foundation, also assured me no one from his outfit had gone to the Marianas, saying, "It's not on our radar screen at all." He was also in error. Daniel Mitchell of the Heritage Foundation was on the journey with Thomas, as was Doug Bandow, a senior fellow at the Cato Institute.

After unpacking his bags, Bandow proceeded to write a lengthy report on the Marianas that was published by CEI. He raved about the islands' "stunning economic success" and warned that imposition of the U.S. minimum wage would be "a serious mistake." The report did not mention that his research trip to the islands was paid for by the Tenorio regime.

Thomas and Mitchell came back from their trip and briefed Representative Phil Crane of Illinois about their findings. Afterwards, Crane announced to the press, "I was impressed by what these well known free-market advocates tell me is the phenomenal success" of the CNMI.

Clint Bolick of the Institute for Justice is another Marianas junketeer. He wrote two fawning articles about the CNMI upon his return, one in *Human Events* and the other in the *Wall Street Journal*. In neither article did Bolick disclose that he had traveled to the CNMI courtesy of Governor Tenorio. The *Human Events* story quoted Bandow, a prior junketeer, in describing the CNMI as an "experimental laboratory of liberty."

It's no wonder that Tenorio told a local newspaper in late 1997 that the CNMI planned to maintain its junket strategy. Even as he spoke, Resources Committee Chairman Don Young was putting together another junket to the Marianas for later in the winter.

Lobbying Ethics: An Oxymoron

It should come as no surprise to learn that when hunting for foreign clients, lobbyists throw their political convictions, to the extent that they have any, straight out the window. Liberal Democrats such as Howard Paster, Clinton's first chief congressional lobbyist, and Frank Mankiewicz, a former aide to Robert Kennedy and ex-head of National Public Radio, now head up Hill & Knowlton, a firm that has represented human rights abusers such as Turkey, Indonesia and China.

Grover Norquist is a staunch right-winger who advises Newt Gingrich and who back in the 1980s helped build public support for the contras, the mujahedin and other dubious "freedom fighters" that were backed by the Reagan administration. As of 1996, Norquist had a $60,000-a-year contract to lobby for UNITA, the Angolan anti-Communist guerrillas headed up by the ghastly Jonas Savimbi. At the same time, Norquist was working for Marxist leader France-Albert Rene in the Seychelles Island. His contract called for him to "promote and strengthen ties between" the U.S. and the Seychelles, and to help "ensure a long-lasting relationship between the two nations, with specific regard to U.S. military activities in the Indian Ocean."

Norquist's ties to the far right were surely of great use to the Seychelles. On its behalf, he met with anti-Communist stalwarts such as Reps. David McIntosh, Ileana Ros-Lehtinen and Randy Tate. He opened doors with the latter with a chintzy campaign contribution of $100. Shortly after making said donation, Norquist met with Tate to urge greater U.S. support for the Seychelles, a country with a population of about 75,000 but, as Norquist would have it, a vitally important American ally.

What's especially curious about Norquist's activities is that in the early 1990s, he had railed against Rene's government and championed oppositionist Sir James Mancham (described by Tucker Carlson in the *New Republic* as "a legendary womanizer with a weakness for treacly poetry"). Norquist changed his tune after Rene put him on the payroll to the tune of $10,000 a month.

Bruce Fein is another lobbyist who will sign on with any client, be it a right-wing terrorist group or a torture-prone outlaw government, if the price is right. The case of Fein also demonstrates how foreign lobbyists bilk their clients for huge sums of money while performing work of little or no value.

A graduate of Harvard Law School, Fein served as associate attorney general under Ronald Reagan between 1981 and 1983 and played a key role in formulating the administration's policies on civil rights, school prayer, abortion and crime. He backed the failed bid to grant tax-exempt status to Bob Jones University, which does not accept black students.

After leaving government, Fein linked up with right-wing think tanks such as the Heritage Foundation and the American Enterprise Institute. He also cashed in on his government experience by lobbying for foreign clients, including Saudi Arabia and Turkey.

Fein hit the jackpot in 1991, when he signed on to represent Mozambique's notorious guerrilla army, RENAMO, which was then seeking to overthrow its country's Marxist government. When Fein came on board, RENAMO's reputation had hit rock bottom. This was just a few years after the State Department had issued a report denouncing the guerrillas for the wholesale slaughter of civilians, using such methods as "shooting executions, knife/ax/bayonet killings, burning alive, beating to death, forced asphyxiation, forced starvation, forced drownings and random shootings."

American support for RENAMO was limited to the looniest sectors of the anti-Communist Christian right. Even the Reagan and Bush administrations kept their distance from RENAMO. So reviled were the group and its president, Afonso Dhlakama, that President Reagan held several face-to-face meetings with Mozambique's leader, Joaquim Chissano, to demonstrate support for his Marxist government!

Fein, however, signed up to flack for Dhlakama's terror army. His chief endeavor appears to have been writing "The Dhlakama Papers," a collection of the wise leader's theoretical musings, and RENAMO's constitution. The latter document was a loose plagiarism of the U.S. Constitution with a few pet projects of Fein's—the death penalty and privatization of state industries—thrown in for good measure.

Fein also obtained invitations for Dhlakama to address the Heritage Foundation and the Republican Study Group. Dhlakama could not meet these commitments because Fein was unable to secure a visa for him to enter the U.S.

Such ineffectual efforts to "elicit support for the democracy initiatives of RENAMO" netted Fein at least $175,000. He received roughly two-thirds of that money in July of 1991, the same month that RENAMO's major "democracy initiative" was beheading civilians while rampaging through northern Mozambique.

In 1996, Fein with equal relish took as a client the Sudan, which was then barred from receiving U.S. foreign aid because of its support for terrorism. Furthermore, Amnesty International reported that the Sudanese government assassinates and tortures its "enemies." Paramilitary forces have kidnapped scores of children, who are believed to be held in domestic slavery by their abductors or taken to camps in remote rural areas, where they are trained for military service. Another common practice of the Sudanese government is to flog "criminals." According to Amnesty, many of the victims are women accused of brewing alcohol and convicted by rubber stamp Public Order Courts.

Explaining away a record like that is a delicate task. According to records on file at the Justice Department, Fein charged his client about $10,000 per month to meet with Congress, the executive branch, newspaper editorial boards and think tanks. His goal was to foster "warming relations" with the U.S., have the Sudan delisted as a supporter of terrorism and urge the U.S. government to lift all sanctions against the country, including prohibitions on military aid. As part of his effort, Fein promised his client to prepare favorable pamphlets, monographs and newspaper articles.

Like RENAMO, the Sudan seems to have gotten little for its money. As of this writing, relations between the U.S. and the Sudan are as bad as ever and the Clinton administration is known to have used the CIA to try to undermine Fein's client with the help of anti-government guerrillas in southern Sudan.

I called Fein to ask why he had chosen to represent such a government. Money, of course, had nothing to do with it; Fein was moved to action to rectify the unfair treatment the Sudan receives in the U.S. "There is a vast amount of misperception about what is going on in the Sudan," he said. "It is not that the republic of the Sudan does not have warts; it does. But I am convinced they are serious about making improvements."

The Lobbyists' Credo: I Cannot Tell the Truth

As with domestic service, many foreign lobbyists first establish their bona fides with a stint in government service. They then use their connections with former government colleagues to further the aims of their clients. "The most important reason that lobbying is so effective is that it operates within a network of personal and professional relationships developed in Washington," says Holly Burkhalter, a Washington-based human rights activist. "When a government hands fists of cash to a lobbyist, the implicit understanding is that it is purchasing access to people who decide foreign aid questions."

A good example of how the old boys network operates comes with Herman Cohen, the Bush administration's assistant secretary of state for African affairs. Cohen now lobbies for some of Africa's cruelest tyrants and also runs the Global Coalition for Africa, a World Bank-linked outfit which promotes austerity across the continent. In promoting himself to one client, Cohen described himself as "a retired American ambassador who has devoted 30 years to diplomatic work in Africa. He has enormous contacts with the highest levels of government and private sector in Africa." In the U.S., continued the pitch, Cohen has "rapid access to high officials who are concerned with African affairs."

In early 1995, Cohen signed a one-year deal with the government of Gabon. Cohen's contract called for him to handle media relations, write a monthly press release and promotional brochure, and prepare a visit to Washington by President El Hadj Omar Bongo. His mission, said the contract, was to present Gabon as a "politically stable and economically successful country," and to "generate awareness on President Bongo and his national and international accomplishments," including the "very concrete process of democratization and democratic reforms brought about under [his leadership]."

Around the time that the deal was finalized, the State Department released its annual report on human rights practices around the globe. According to Cohen's former colleagues at State, the government of Gabon was responsible "for many confirmed extrajudicial killings," and torture in President Bongo's homeland was routine: "Eyewitnesses reported seeing prisoners tied to chairs, doused with ice water, or made to crawl on their stomachs over gravel or sun-baked asphalt. There were other credible reports of security forces extracting confessions by beating the soles of prisoners' feet or by bending or twisting fingers."

As to the "very concrete process of democratization" that has taken place under Bongo—in power since 1967—the State Department report said that a December 1993 election in which Bongo triumphed with 51 percent of the vote, was "marred by serious irregularities," including a secret vote count that excluded all but government observers. In Bongo's home region of Haut Ogoue, the number of votes cast for the Supreme Leader was greater than the population reported by the 1993 census.

Not long after Cohen began his work for Gabon's supreme leader, it was disclosed that a number of Parisian prostitutes were suing Bongo's tailor, who procured their services for the dictator without revealing that he is HIV-positive. Bongo paid up to $15,000 per night for his prostitutes. Cohen also charges stiff fees for his services. His contract called for payments of $300,000.

Shilling for Nigeria

Bongo is but an amateur despot next to Nigerian ruler Gen. Sani Abacha. In 1993, Abacha annulled elections won by an opposition leader, Moshood Abiola, and promptly threw the victor in jail. Abiola's wife was later murdered by unidentified gunmen on the streets of Lagos. In 1995, Abacha's regime executed Ken Saro-Wiwa and eight other human rights activists.

Following the execution, President Clinton expressed outrage and promised that he would take tough steps to force change in Nigeria. During the following year a host of Washington lobby and PR shops were paid approximately $1 million to help ensure that Abacha would not be unduly inconvenienced by the U.S. government. Among the firms who took money from the Nigerian hangman were the Washington Public Affairs Group, which was paid $10,000 monthly to seek "to renew the suspended U.S. program to train the Nigerian military," and Symms, Lehn & Associates, a company headed by the illustrious former senator from the State of Idaho, Stephen Symms. It was paid hundreds of thousands of dollars annually to provide "consultative and representational services in the area of American foreign trade laws, regulations and policy programs."

Down deeper in the muck is Washington & Christian, a black firm with close ties to the Democratic Party. Between 1993 and 1996, it was paid $5 million by Abacha's regime.

Not long after Abiola was arrested Washington & Christian produced a report for journalists and members of Congress titled "The Road to Democracy." This brazen document claimed that Abiola's "election was not 'free and fair' and did not reflect the will of the Nigerian people. Prior to the election," the document continued, "massive fraudulent acts occurred which could not have been apparent on the actual date of the election, and therefore not known to either the Nigerian election monitors who thought the elections were 'free and fair' based solely on their observations that day." This is curious since the military announced it would not honor the vote almost as soon as it became apparent that Abiola had won. The report also stated that the Nigerian military "had not only the authority but the duty to annul the June 12, 1993 elections."

The Washington & Christian report concedes that arrests by the military had regrettably taken place, but added that most of those imprisoned had been involved in "activities designed to incite Nigerian citizens and create conflicts." In the same vein, the government has been forced to crush press freedom because "developments in the country necessitated certain actions in order to preserve the peace and maintain the stability of the country....The action taken against certain newspapers was taken not as a result of criticism of the Government, but as a result of the anti-state position taken by these newspapers."

A few months after this revolting piece of work, Robert Washington, a partner in the firm, sent out a letter to members of Congress describing dictator Abacha as a devoted democrat. Washington said that when all the facts were marshaled and carefully considered, he was "confident that you and the world will be convinced of the fact, as I am, that democracy will again thrive in Nigeria." Washington also promised to keep Congress posted on the status of Abiola, whose insistence that he had been rightfully elected Washington described as "offenses against the state." Four years after Washington wrote this optimistic assessment, Nigeria remains a dungeon and Abiola languishes in prison. (It's gratifying to note that Washington & Christian was stiffed for the final $1.3 million due for its work. As a result, the company was forced to lay off a number of employees and in 1997 was confronted with a severe cash crunch.)

Nigeria has also received aid and succor in the U.S. Congress, including from the quarters of Sen. Carole Moseley-Braun. Because she is the only black senator, Moseley-Braun has been avidly courted by Lagos. She traveled there in August of 1996 as a guest of state and came back carrying a letter for President Clinton from Abacha. Accompanying her on this journey was her former fiancé and campaign manager, Kgosie Matthews, who has worked as a lobbyist for Nigeria. Moseley-Braun did not meet with any opposition leaders but did squeeze in a pleasant chat with Col. Dauda Musa Komo, the man who supervised the execution of Saro-Wiwa.

This was Moseley-Braun's second trip to Nigeria. Back in 1992 she skipped orientation for new senators in Washington and traveled to Lagos, also in the company of Matthews. Her fiancé's hiring as a lobbyist for the Nigerian generals followed that visit.

Moseley-Braun has led the pro-Nigeria caucus in Congress, testifying against a sanctions bill that was killed in the Senate Foreign Relations Committee. In early-1997, a group of pro-democracy Nigerians traveled to Washington to meet with members and staffers, including Chailandu Pegues of Moseley-Braun's office. Notes from the meeting taken by the Nigerians say, "We went from a provocative strategy session to a bout of strategic provocation." The low point came when Pegues told the visitors that his boss was "outraged" by the execution of Saro-Wiwa but that Nigeria's legal system was an internal matter except in cases of gross violations of human rights. The execution of Saro-Wiwa and the other eight activists was "too close to call," Pegues said.

Abacha has gotten good value for his money, with the Clinton administration huffing and puffing about its concern for human rights in Nigeria but never imposing more than token sanctions against the regime. The administration is more concerned with the health of oil companies with big investments in Nigeria, such as Shell, Chevron, Texaco and Gulf. Shell alone makes about $300 million a year in profits off Nigeria and has begun work on a $4 billion natural gas joint venture with the military regime. As one administration official intimately involved in the Nigeria situation told a group of human rights activists during an off-the-record talk, "There is plenty of oil [available on world markets], but there's only so much Bonney Light." He was referring to Nigeria's coveted crude, which is extremely pure and economical to refine.

Mid-level Tyrants: A Lobbyist's Niche Market

No chapter about foreign lobbying would be complete without paying tribute to Edward J. van Kloberg III. Even within the amoral world of Washington lobbying, van Kloberg stands out for handling clients that no one else will touch. In an unsuccessful effort to establish his ethical bottom line, *Spy* magazine in 1992 dreamed up the German People's Alliance. The group's fictitious representative, Sabina Hofer, telephoned van Kloberg to see if he'd be interested in promoting the Alliance's neo-Nazi agenda on Capitol Hill. A few key demands were banning immigration into Germany, "increasing our voice in the U.S. Congress to counter the pro-Jewish claque," and reclaiming Poland.

Informed that the group had up to $1 million to spend, the lobbyist expressed keen interest in obtaining the contract. "I believe in many of the tenets that you believe in," van Kloberg told Hofer. "So we are not very far apart, my dear."

Van Kloberg's real life clients have included dictators Saddam Hussein of Iraq, Mobutu Sese Seko of Zaire, Nicolae Ceausescu of Romania, and Samuel Doe of Liberia. Van Kloberg's well-remunerated exertions on behalf of the last two came to an abrupt end when they were murdered by their countrymen following long periods of brutal rule.

Van Kloberg specializes in representing mid-level African tyrants. In the fall of 1990, he arranged the D.C. visit of Rwanda's then-President Juvenal Habyarimana. In a series of activities, including a posh reception at the Grand Hotel, van Kloberg touted the stern but wise leader's great popularity among the Rwandan masses. Unfortunately, the trip was cut short when a guerrilla army seeking to topple Habyarimana invaded Rwanda from neighboring Uganda.

With the war causing serious public relations difficulties, the Rwandan regime in late 1990 signed a new one-month deal with van Kloberg. For the sum of $11,000, the lobbyist was to help Ambassador H.E. Aloys Uwimana "counterbalance any negative influence [that human rights groups] might exert on U.S. policy."

Van Kloberg's contract called for him to promote "measures undertaken by the Government of Rwanda in the areas of environmental conservation and wildlife management." America's adoration of Rwanda's threatened mountain gorillas—immortalized in the 1988 film "Gorillas in the Mist"—made this an especially clever strategy, and one which helped Rwanda extract U.S. monies for conservation projects. That was the sole interest of President Habyarimana, whose own relatives were widely believed to be involved in the international trafficking of gorillas.

Van Kloberg also arranged a 1991 U.S. tour for King Mswati III and a delegation of leaders from Swaziland, a corrupt regime which had close ties to leaders of South Africa's apartheid government. The group was given a "VIP tour of the Pentagon" and of the National Aquarium in Baltimore, visited Colt Industry's indoor shooting range in Hartford, and then flew to the Martin Luther King Center in Atlanta, where former United Nations ambassador Andrew Young offered a special viewing of "From Montgomery to Memphis," a documentary

(c) Vince Heptig, 1997, from *A Mayan Struggle*

A 12-year-old's story—one of 140,000 Guatemalan civilians murdered since 1954: The remains of a 12-year-old boy still have the rope tied around his hands, contradicting the army's version that this death was combat-related. This child's skeleton bears a trademark of the Guatemalan army: the skull shattered by a gunshot wound to the back of the head. Lobbyist Edward J. van Kloberg III accepted $75,000 from a Guatemalan special interest group to polish the country's human rights image.

about the civil rights movement.

A former congressional staffer who worked on African affairs says that van Kloberg rarely was of great service to his clients. "He tries to be suave and debonair, but comes across as paternalistic and patronizing," she recalls. "His views on Africans were offensive and racist. I could never figure out why anyone would hire him."

Van Kloberg has also represented a number of Latin regimes, including El Salvador, Nicaragua, Haiti, and Guatemala. The latter government is in perennial need of PR help due to its abysmal human rights record and appalling social inequalities. Since a CIA-organized coup in 1954 overthrew an elected, left-leaning government and set the stage for decades of rule by terror, the military has murdered 140,000 civilians. In an interview a few years ago in the *Harvard International Review*, former defense minister Gen. Hector Gramajo described the army's counterinsurgency strategy as providing "development for 70 percent of the population while we kill 30 percent."

In January of 1995, the Foundation for the Development of Guatemala (FUNDESA)—a front group of ultra-conservative business leaders who work closely with their government — contracted van Kloberg to conduct a three-month, $75,000 public relations campaign. FUNDESA was especially anxious for van Kloberg to "balance the PR campaign implemented by ... sympathizers" of Jennifer Harbury, the American woman who shortly before the contract was signed had begun conducting hunger strikes in Guatemala and in the U.S., as a means of pressuring both governments to reveal what they knew about the murder of her husband, Efrain Bamaca Velasquez, a guerrilla fighter who disappeared in 1992 after being captured by the armed forces.

In return for the $75,000, van Kloberg's firm drafted and placed letters to the editor—signed by Guatemala's ambassador

©Vince Heptig, December 12, 1997

If only they'd had money for a lobbyist! Acul villagers look on as members of the Foundation for Forensic Anthropology of Guatemala meticulously uncover bones from a mass grave. Over the years, relatives of the deceased and members of the judiciary have been threatened with reprisal, delaying discovery of these clandestine cemeteries. The Acul exhumations were documented by digital photos transmitted daily to Amnesty International USA. Along with many other beltway lobbyists, van Kloberg had no problem shilling for the killers.

to the U.S., Edmond Mulet, and describing supposed strides toward democracy taking place under the current government—in the *New York Times*, the *Miami Herald*, and a few other newspapers. Van Kloberg's firm also produced *Guatemala News*, a three-page newsletter targeting Congress, the press and business leaders. The publication informed readers that guerrilla groups battling the government had been committing heinous abuses "against the civilian population," such as the imposition of road blocks, collection of "war taxes" from landowners, and "attacks perpetrated against the electricity grid."

Guatemala News somehow failed to mention that a few weeks prior to its publication date, a U.N. Verification Mission released a report on human rights in Guatemala which detailed 27 extrajudicial executions, 8 attempted executions, 10 cases of torture and 72 death threats—all between December of 1994 and February of 1995. The U.N. concluded that the Guatemalan government "has not guaranteed people's right to safety and security, or to freedom from torture or cruel, inhumane or degrading treatment."

Unfortunately for van Kloberg and FUNDESA, the timing for a PR offensive was poor. In mid-March, halfway through the contract's life span, Rep. Robert Torricelli of New Jersey revealed to the press that Guatemalan soldiers on the CIA payroll had murdered Harbury's husband. Shortly thereafter it was also disclosed that the CIA's Guatemalan assets had been responsible for the 1990 murder of Michael DeVine, an American who ran an inn in the highlands and who apparently had discovered army units illegally logging mahogany. These disclosures produced a flood of denunciations in the American press—which had largely turned a blind eye to the previous forty years of carnage.

Van Kloberg defends flacking for thugs by arguing that lawyers represent both guilty and innocent clients, and that he should not be held to a different standard. "In the American tradition, every person—every nation—is entitled to representation," van Kloberg once wrote in an op-ed article for the *Journal of Commerce*. "[That includes] those who have been condemned for various offenses." This contention is wholly specious. Unlike suspected criminals, who are locked up pending trial, Van Kloberg's clients hold the reins of power in their nations and pay him to help ensure that they are never held accountable in a court of law. Lawyers don't provide favors or make campaign contributions to judges on behalf of their clients. The equivalent of van Kloberg's representation of despots would be to give lawyers of homicidal defendants private audiences with jurors.

In the capital, van Kloberg's shameful client list has in no way diminished his stature. "One of lobbying's true characters," the *Washingtonian* called him in a flattering profile in 1993. "He maintains friendly relations with Washington's powerful, and his dinners for legislators and opinion-makers at the Jockey Club are legendary."

Fronting for Dictators:
Corporate America Takes Charge

During recent years, U.S. corporations with overseas investment have frequently stepped in to handle lobbying campaign for foreign governments. Having American firms at the forefront of a lobbying effort helps fosters the illusion that maintaining warm ties with corrupt despots is good for the American economy and therefore in the national interest. It also avoids charges that foreign governments are unduly seeking to influence U.S. politics.

One beneficiary of such corporate lobbying is the military regime in Burma which rules by terror and keeps opposition leaders, including Nobel Peace Prize winner Aung San Suu Kyi, under virtual house arrest. As one of the most reviled

regimes in the world, Burma is keenly aware of the need to pol-
ish its image in the U.S. However, spin control efforts orches-
trated by the military regime—known as the State Law and
Order Council, or SLORC—have backfired badly.

In 1992, the junta hired—surprise!—Edward van Kloberg to
lobby on its behalf. Van Kloberg helped arrange meetings
between Burma's ambassador to the U.S., U Thaung, and 23
members of Congress. However, the SLORC was apparently
embarrassed by the negative media coverage that followed the
deal. It summarily dismissed van Kloberg and stiffed him for
$5,000. The lobbyist, who previously lavished praise on U
Thaung, soon began publicly referring to him as a "little shit."

Following the van Kloberg debacle, the SLORC withdrew
from the scene, leaving the job of lobbying Congress to
American firms with investments in Burma. Many companies
have pulled out of Burma in response to pressure from U.S. sol-
idarity groups, including Disney and PepsiCo, so the sordid
task of selling Burma to the U.S. government and public land-
ed squarely on the shoulders of oil giant UNOCAL. That company has desperately sought to head off economic sanctions
against Burma, a step which could jeopardize its $1.2 billion
share in an oil pipeline joint venture with the dictatorship in
Rangoon, the French firm Total and the government of
Thailand.

UNOCAL's lobbying campaign has had significant success.
In 1996, Congress passed a bill requiring the Clinton administration to impose stiff sanctions against Burma if the junta
stepped up repression against the opposition. The administration steadfastly refused to act, even though Amnesty
International described 1996 as the worst year for human
rights in Burma since 1988, when the military seized power
and slaughtered 3,000 people. Finally, in mid-1997, Clinton
imposed sanctions on Burma but he did not force UNOCAL
to pull out of the pipeline joint venture.

UNOCAL insists that the best way to promote human rights in Burma is to have other U.S. firms join it there. "Engagement and investment are the keys to starting a Third World country on the road to political reform," says a PR statement the firm helped draft. "Isolation is exactly the wrong approach." The company's strategy of speaking only in vague terms about the supposed benefits of "engagement" is a wise one, since it's hard to see how participation in a huge joint venture with a cabal of military thugs could somehow enhance the cause of democracy. And UNOCAL quite naturally prefers to avoid discussing the messy details of its involvement in Burma, such as the company's decision to provide the cash-strapped dictatorship with a $7 million credit for fertilizer, to be paid back only after the pipeline comes on line.

To promote its ludicrous arguments, UNOCAL recruited a number of heavy hitters, including Tom Korologos, a prominent GOP lobbyist who served as one of Bob Dole's top campaign advisers. During Congressional debate in 1996, Korologos put heavy pressure on Republicans who were considering voting for a bill sponsored by Sens. Daniel Patrick Moynihan of New York and Mitch McConnell of Kentucky that would have immediately slapped sanctions on Rangoon. Just before the crucial vote, Korologos hosted several dinners aimed at raising funds for the key swing voters and used those occasions to discreetly raise the issue of Burma with the grateful members of Congress. With Korologos's help, UNOCAL managed to narrowly defeat the Moynihan-McConnell bill. That cleared the way for passage of a loophole-ridden measure that Clinton later clung to as a justification for inaction.

UNOCAL also sought to influence public opinion, selecting the Washington PR firm of Edelman Worldwide to handle this task. To drum up positive press, Edelman associate Katie Connorton courted university professors. In a January 31, 1997 letter to one academic, Connorton said that UNOCAL "would like the opportunity to provide you and your colleagues with an overview of how the Yadana project is helping...[bring] high-paying jobs, economic development, and socio-economic assistance." Such a briefing, she suggested, would be perfect fodder for an article about the oil company's heartwarming deeds in Burma.

Among UNOCAL's most effective allies are two "nonpartisan" beltway outfits which have helped arrange a number of congressional junkets to Burma. The Asia Pacific Exchange Foundation is headed by a right-wing reserve army general, Richard Quick, and has sponsored delegations to China and Singapore in addition to Burma. In 1996, the foundation paid for 18 members of Congress to visit Asia, at a cost of $93,301, the fourth-largest amount spent by any sponsor of Hill junkets.

In December of 1996, the Foundation paid for four Republicans in Congress—Tom DeLay of Texas, Bill Paxon of New York, Dennis Hastert of Illinois and Deborah Pryce of Ohio—to travel to Burma. The quartet met with army commander Gen. Maung Aye and other military officials on December 10, International Human Rights Day. A photo-op of that gathering was prominently featured in the *New Light of Myanmar*, a state-run newspaper.

The U.S. representatives did not meet with opposition leaders during their visit but did find time to fly—on a military plane—to Pagan, a lovely town surrounded by thousands of temples and pagodas, and where villagers were forcibly removed to keep them away from tourists and foreign reporters. The members of Congress also visited the pipeline facilities, this being of particular interest to DeLay and Hastert as UNOCAL makes generous contributions to their political campaigns.

The Burma/Myanmar Forum is run by Frances Zwenig, a former staffer to Sen. John Kerry of Massachusetts, who describes itself as "a key information source for those interested in developing the United States-Burma relationship." The Forum has sponsored several trips to Burma, including a February 1997 junket for five carefully selected Hill staffers. These included Deanna Okun from the office of Sen. Frank Murkowski, perhaps the most rabidly pro-oil member of Congress, and Dan Bob from the office of Sen. William Roth, head of the Senate Finance Committee, which oversees sanctions.

Neither Quick nor Zwenig will reveal their organizations' financial backers. However, David Garcia, a spokesman at UNOCAL's headquarters in Los Angeles, acknowledged that the oil company subsidizes both operations. He would not say in what amount. "These are independent organizations which pursue their mandates in an objective manner," said Garcia. "We have every right to support them. Asia is a major market for us."

The beauty of the arrangement from UNOCAL's point of view is that both the Asia Pacific Exchange Foundation and the Burma/Myanmar Forum are nonprofit groups. Hence, in making a donation, UNOCAL not only obtains their lobbying services but gets a tax deduction as well.

Corporate America's Democracy Program in Mexico: Kill the Zapatistas

As seen in the Burma campaign, a common feature to the business-led lobbying campaigns is the allegation that Corporate America cares deeply about democracy and human rights but believes that economic "engagement" with anti-democratic governments is the best way to bring about change. Love of dollars, not democracy, is the motivating force behind corporate lobbying for increased trade and economic ties with human rights abusing regimes. "Not many multinational businessmen care if the country they locate in is a democracy or a dictatorship," says Kevin Kearns of the U.S. Business and

Industrial Council, one of the few corporate groups that has sought to restrict trade with outlaw governments. "Their job is to make money. It's not a group that you often find at the fore-front of democratic movements."

An amazingly frank expression of Corporate America's real views on democracy is contained in a January 13, 1995, memo on Mexico drafted by Chase Bank's Emerging Markets group and sent to a group of its top clients. The four-page report went out three weeks after the Mexican economy collapsed along with the peso, with the ensuing crisis—resolved only by a $50 billion bail-out mission organized through the Clinton admin-istration—threatening one of Wall Street's hottest "emerging markets."

Bankers are normally prudent with their utterances on political matters, but Chase was panic- stricken at the prospect of huge losses—at the time it held about $1.5 million in Mexican securities and ranked third among U.S. banks in the provision of peso-denominated loans and financial services to Mexican companies. Under these circumstances, Chase issued what amounted to Wall Street's program for returning the situ-ation to the status quo ante: army terror and fixed elections.

Very early on, the Bank's memo called for a return to "polit-ical stability." "Stability" is banker speak for conditions favor-able to making money—i.e. a cowed labor force and low wages—and promotes that most precious of commodities, "investor confidence," which was menaced in Mexico by three factors which the Chase memo hastened to identify.

First was the Zapatista revolt in the southern province of Chiapas. To address this problem, Chase proposed blunt action: "While Chiapas, in our opinion, does not pose a funda-mental threat to Mexican political stability, it is perceived to be so by many in the investment community. The government will need to eliminate the Zapatistas to demonstrate their effective control of the national territory and security policy."

Less than a month after the bank circulated this document, President Ernesto Zedillo unleashed the Mexican army against the Zapatistas in a brief assault, one of whose major purposes appears to have been the display of resolve demanded by Chase and other Wall Street players.

Second was the awful possibility that democracy in Mexico could be permitted to function, thus disturbing the 65-year uninterrupted rule of the Institutional Revolutionary Party, the party of property and of foreign investors. Here, too, the Bank had a solution handy: "The Zedillo administration will need to consider carefully whether or not to allow opposition victories if fairly won at the ballot box. To deny legitimate electoral victories by the opposition will be a serious setback in the President's electoral strategy. But a failure to retain PRI control runs the risk of splitting the government party."

Third was the dreadful chance that long-docile labor unions would have the effrontery to seek a decent wage for their members. Even though the economic crisis would make it virtually impossible for "the average Mexican worker to purchase the bare necessities of life," Chase urged Zedillo to hold firm, as "yielding to worker demands" would only aggravate the economic situation.

The author of the Emerging Market Group's grisly memo was Riordan Roett, director of Latin American Studies at the Johns Hopkins School of Advanced International Studies, who had taken a leave of absence while serving as a Chase advisor. Known as a conservative but rational sort in academic circles, Roett' seems to have hardened in his views after he went to work full-time for Wall Street, in the grand homicidal tradition of such academic policy makers as Walt Rostow and Henry Kissinger.

Not content with dispensing this bloodthirsty recipe for Mexican recovery, Chase dispatched Roett on a lobbying mission to Washington, where he briefed senators such as Bob

Dole and Trent Lott,advised State Department officials, and addressed hundreds of political and financial leaders at a January 11, 1997, seminar organized by the Center for Strategic and International Studies.

The New China Lobby

Nowhere has big business expended so much time and effort as in its sophisticated and expensive lobbying campaign to retain most favored nation (MFN) trade status for China. The China campaign shows how foreign policy is driven by commercial interests, and provides a look at the full arsenal of Corporate America's lobbying weaponry.

The stakes in the MFN battle are enormous. Bilateral trade between the U.S. and China hit $55 billion in 1996 and U.S. investment in China climbed from $358 million in 1990 to $25 billion in 1996.

Trade with Beijing has grown especially fast since 1994, the year that President Clinton formally delinked China's trade status from its human rights record. During that same period, the human rights situation has markedly deteriorated.

Before Clinton's move, China did slightly improve its human rights record under U.S. pressure. Between 1991 and 1994, Congress threatened to cut off China's most favored nation (MFN) status unless it eased up on human rights abuses. During that period, China released a large number of political prisoners, invited the United Nations to visit Tibet and opened talks with the Red Cross about granting the organization access to political detainees.

All improvements came to a swift halt after Clinton let up the pressure. Mike Jendrzjczyk, an Asia specialist at Human Rights Watch, says, "The fact that the Clinton administration has put business at the top of the agenda and human rights at the bottom has fueled the perception in Beijing that it can use the lure of its market to blunt any international pressure or criticism."

China has had MFN since 1980 but, because it does not allow its citizens freedom of emigration as called for by the Jackson-Vanik Act, it must have its trade privileges re-authorized by the president every year. Congress can block the decision if both chambers pass a resolution of disapproval within 60 days.

As of 1990, only a few dozen firms were actively lobbying on China's behalf. Today the Business Coalition for U.S.-China Trade has 800 members, mostly big companies but including trade associations and the Business Roundtable, the National Association of Manufacturers and the Chamber of Commerce. The Coalition's growth was spurred by the election of Clinton, who had criticized Bush for "coddling dictators" and promised a tougher line towards Beijing. Of course, Clinton has turned out to be as friendly to China as his predecessor. He has rubber-stamped China's MFN renewal and in 1994, at the direct behest of the business lobby, formally de-linked China's trade status from its human rights record.

In Congress, the situation is far different. Everyone from Senator Jesse Helms of North Carolina, who views Beijing as Red Central after the fall of the Soviet Union, to Rep. Nancy Pelosi of California, a liberal Democrat and critic of China's human rights record, have opposed MFN for China.

China itself has done little to directly counter such critics. A few years ago Beijing retained a variety of blue chip lobby shops but the only firm it now pays to curry favor in the capital is Jones, Day, Reavis and Pogue. Beijing has also funneled money to American non-profit groups that pay for members of Congress to visit China.

In 1996, in what emerged as a major component of the Clinton administration's "Donorgate" scandal, China reportedly funneled $1 million to its embassy in Washington and to five consulates, as part of what *Newsweek* called "a remarkably clear and detailed blueprint...to influence American politicians

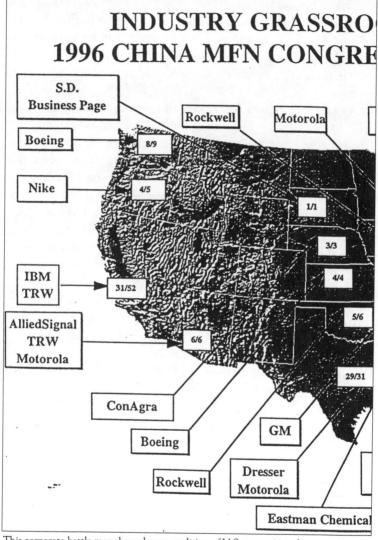

This corporate battle map shows how a coalition of U.S. transnational corporations mobilized at the grassroots to win most-favored nation trading status for China. It was obtained by the Madison, Wisconsin, investigative quarterly *PR Watch*. The headline reads: INDUSTRIAL GRASSROOTS INITIATIVE
1996 CHINA MFN CONGRESSIONAL OUTCOME

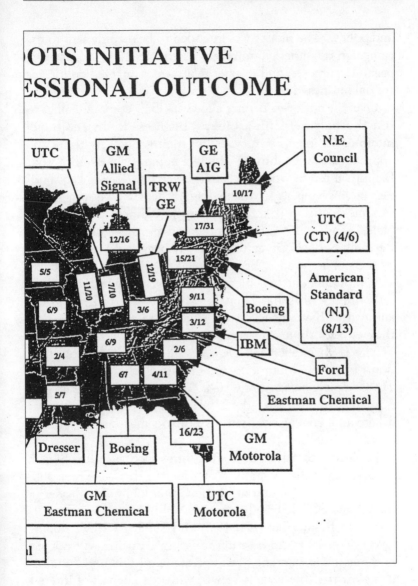

OTS INITIATIVE
ESSIONAL OUTCOME

UTC

GM
Allied
Signal

TRW
GE

GE
AIG

N.E.
Council

10/17

UTC
(CT) (4/6)

17/31

12/16

15/21

American
Standard
(NJ)
(8/13)

5/5

11/20

7/10

12/19

9/11

Boeing

6/9

3/6

3/12

IBM

2/4

6/9

2/6

Ford

6/7

4/11

Eastman Chemical

5/7

16/23

GM
Motorola

Dresser

Boeing

GM
Eastman Chemical

UTC
Motorola

and policy." The money was intended to be secretly sent to the campaign treasuries of prominent political figures, used for propaganda purposes, and to offer relatives of targeted politicians special business deals in China.

Overall, however, Beijing allows its U.S. corporate allies to run the beltway China lobby. "Business lobbyists [have] informed Chinese Embassy staff of their general strategies and approaches, but Chinese officials apparently decided that Beijing's interests would be better served by allowing U.S. business groups to speak for themselves, rather than be seen as part of some coalition of forces led by the Chinese Embassy officials," reads a 1997 report prepared by the Congressional Research Service. Given the "strongly negative" view of China by the public, it adds, Beijing's low-key approach is "probably an appropriate one to achieve China's overall objective."

While Beijing has been low-key on the Hill, Chinese authorities have made crystal clear to U.S. executives that they expect them to stand up for China in Washington. "There is an implicit but clear reward-and-punishment equation," says Ross Munro, co-author with Richard Bernstein of *The Coming Conflict with China.* "Company investments may not fare so well if they don't take China's side in the policy debate and, conversely, their investments may fare better than ever if they do."

Prodded into action by Beijing, firms such as Allied-Signal, AT&T, Caterpillar, Cargill, Motorola and the Big Three auto makers are at the forefront of the China lobby. The leader of the pack is Seattle-based Boeing, which sold one in ten of its planes to Beijing between 1993 and 1995. In 1996, Boeing held one of its board meetings in China. Boeing will not say how much it is spending to win permanent MFN for China but it is clear that the issue is viewed with the keenest of interest back in Seattle. "Throwing the entire relationship on the table every year just doesn't make sense," says Thomas Tripp, a

Boeing spokesman. "It's like entering into a marriage every year."

Led by Boeing, the corporate lobby has pooled its resources to support groups such as the U.S.-China Business Council, which sports a $4 million budget and has offices in Washington and Beijing, the Emergency Committee for American Trade, whose members worldwide sales top $1 trillion, and the Business Coalition for U.S.-China Trade. The latter, the primary business voice in the MFN debate, is run out of the offices of Hogan & Hartson, a leading beltway lobby shop.

Needless to say, the China lobby has plenty of access on the Hill, thanks to the roughly $20 million in campaign donations that it made in the year prior to the 1996 Congressional vote on MFN. Grateful members of Congress, including Reps. John Boehner of Ohio and David Dreier of California, showed their appreciation by meeting directly with business reps to plot the MFN strategy. On January 7, 1997, the first day of the 105th Congress, Rep. Doug Bereuter of Nebraska introduced a bill that would have eliminated the MFN process. Instead, Bereuter—whose election campaigns are also generously financed by the China lobby—would automatically grant MFN to all members of the World Trade Organization, to which Beijing has an application pending.

But the China lobby's biggest friend in Congress is Sen. Dianne Feinstein of California. Feinstein's romance with China dates to the 1970s, when she was mayor of San Francisco and became close friends with Jiang Zemin, then mayor of Beijing and now China's president. In explaining her interest in U.S.-China relations, Feinstein has said, "In my last life I was Chinese."

It's not possible to confirm this but even if true, Feinstein's passion for Beijing is more likely linked to the fact that her husband in her current life, merchant banker Richard Blum, has substantial business and real estate interests in China. Blum manages $750 million in investments for about 70 companies, with a large chunk of that amount tied up in China. Blum is also a director of Shanghai Pacific Partners, a major import-export firm. In 1994, Feinstein led the effort to renew MFN for Beijing at a time that her husband was preparing to invest $150 million of his clients' money, along with $2 to $3 million of his own, in China.

The China lobby has augmented its firepower by deploying a fleet of lobbyists to directly pressure Congress. The precise size of the K Street battalion is impossible to determine but it numbers in the hundreds and includes lobbyists from practically every influential shop in town. In addition to Hogan & Hartson, the China lobby has retained Patton, Boggs—which assigned eight lobbyists to the MFN campaign, including Tommy Boggs and Michael Brown, son of late Commerce Secretary Ron Brown—Hill and Knowlton, headed by Howard Paster; and Manatt, Phelps & Phillips, past home to ex-Commerce Secretary Mickey Kantor. These four firms alone took in at least $160,000 in 1996 to lobby on the MFN issue.

At the state level, the China lobby has adopted the model used during the NAFTA campaign, with corporate "captains" assigned to lead the effort in different states and regions. To avoid creating the perception—though an entirely accurate one—that the China lobby is controlled by big business, the captains have set up "grassroots" coalitions of small- and medium-sized local businesses to meet with community groups, the media and political leaders. The companies have also pressured their contractors and subcontractors to write to Congress on China's behalf.

The strategy has been highly successful, as seen during the 1996 congressional vote on MFN. In Michigan, a coalition led by General Motors and Allied Signal won the votes of all but four of the state's 16-member House delegation, including John Conyers, one of the most liberal members of Congress. Of the eight representatives from Washington state, Boeing's backyard, only conservative Rep. Linda Smith opposed MFN for Beijing, in large part due to China's record on forced abortions. In New York, Nita Lowey came on board the China train after being personally lobbied by IBM while Harlem's Charles Rangel was won over by Wall Street. In Florida, Motorola and United Technologies lined up support from 16 of the state's 23 votes in the House. In Texas, Dresser Industries and Motorola brought home 29 of the state's 31 votes in the House.

Kissinger: The Nobel Laureate of Lobbying

The China lobby also counts on support from dozens of former government officials—from the commercial, diplomatic and military establishment—who write pro-China op-ed pieces, send letters to members of Congress and personally lobby on the Hill. Many of these officials have money at stake in China, though this rarely is noted when they shill for Beijing.

Former Secretary of State Henry Kissinger now heads Kissinger Associates, the consulting firm which opens doors for U.S. companies seeking business in China (and other Third World nations). In 1997, Disney hired Kissinger to smooth ruffled feathers with China over the company's production of *Kundun*, a film that spoke favorably of the Dalai Lama, the spiritual leader of Chinese-occupied Tibet. Chinese anger over the movie threatened Disney's plans to open a theme park outside of Beijing.

Following the massacre at Tiananmen, Kissinger appeared on ABC News and voiced enthusiastic support for the Chinese regime's actions. In justifying the blood bath, Kissinger argued that no government in the world should be expected to tolerate protesters' occupation of a public square for a lengthy period of time.

Former U.S. ambassador to China Leonard Woodcock advises Bell Helicopter and Chrysler on their China operations. In 1996, David Rothkopf left the Commerce Department, where he promoted trade with China, to take up residence as managing director of Kissinger Associates, where he performs the same function. Lionel Olmer, a Commerce undersecretary for international trade under Ronald Reagan and now counsel to the board of U.S.-China Business Council, advises American firms that export to China while simultaneously lobbying against restrictions on high-tech exports to Beijing.

Two especially active friends of China are Al Haig and Brent Scowcroft. The former, a secretary of state under Ronald Reagan, has helped United Technologies work the China market and also serves as "honorary senior advisor" to a Chinese firm called Cosco, which is seeking to take over closed Navy facilities in Long Beach, California. Haig furiously lobbied Congress during Congressional debate on MFN in 1996, though his apparent lack of mental equilibrium—which so frightened the public during his years of public service that Haig was in large measure responsible for producing the Nuclear Freeze movement—did not serve Beijing well. "Haig aggressively berated anyone who dared oppose his views and scoffed at their intelligence," says an aide to Rep. Chris Cox of California. "When my boss suggested that Taiwan be admitted to the WTO ahead of China, he went absolutely ballistic."

As a member of the National Security Council, Scowcroft in 1989 traveled to Beijing shortly after the crackdown at Tiananmen Square for consultations with Chinese leaders (who commemorated his arrival by pummeling a group of student demonstrators). After leaving government, Scowcroft went to Kissinger Associates and now heads his own consulting firm, The Scowcroft Group, which develops "market entry strategies" for companies seeking overseas opportunities. In October of 1996, Scowcroft traveled to Beijing, joining Chubb Corporation CEO Dean O'Hare at a meeting with Premier Li Peng. According to an account in the Chinese press, Li "expressed his appreciation for the prolonged efforts Scowcroft has made in helping to develop Sino-U.S. relations," while Scowcroft assured his host that he was "willing to make further efforts" for that cause. Scowcroft also sits on the board of at least two corporations with big interests in China, Northrop-Grumman and Qualcomm, and is a trustee of the business-funded Asia Pacific Exchange Foundation, a right-wing beltway outfit that promotes closer ties with Beijing.

None of this has stopped Scowcroft from offering himself up as a dispassionate observer of the China scene. He testifies on the Hill about the importance of close ties to Beijing, briefs members of Congress on the MFN issue at the invitation of the Heritage Foundation and other conservative think tanks, and speaks at public events where he reiterates those positions.

Bending Public Perceptions

The China lobby has not only targeted Congress. With polls showing Americans overwhelmingly put human rights above trade with China, the Fortune 500 has spent lavishly to secretly influence public opinion. "The companies [with big investments in China] all face PR difficulties," Kenneth DeWoskin, a professor at the University of Michigan Business School and consultant to several automobile companies that do business in China, says in explaining the campaign. "That requires an ongoing effort to educate the public and make people feel positive about U.S. investment there."

Allan Myer of Hill and Knowlton helped coordinate the PR whitewash by retaining pro-China academics to draft newspaper op-ed articles and speak at public events. He also helped produce Panglossian brochures that laud China and urge an expansion of U.S. trade with Beijing, as well as a video called

"New Faces of China," which the *New York Times* described as "a remarkably dewy-eyed depiction of China—no repression of dissidents, no sales of automatic weapons to gangs in Los Angeles, no nuclear proliferation, but plenty of Chinese enjoying American goods." According to DeWoskin, the companies paying for the campaign distribute such material "through their normal PR channels," show them internally to workers and middle managers, and release them in their home communities. Some of the promotional material has even been distributed to educational organizations and individual teachers.

A final element in the China lobby's campaign is the sponsorship of various public forums where the U.S.-China relationship is discussed. In April of 1997, the Council on Foreign Relations held a two-day conference, "From Bicycles to Beepers: The Politics and Economics of Business in China," complete with workshops on investment possibilities and how to set up joint ventures. Much of the money for the affair was provided by U.S. firms with investments in China.

AT&T, the Ford Foundation, GM, Boeing, Cargill and Dupont paid for a conference on China held at Columbia University in November of 1996. Featured speakers included John Whitehead, head of a financial firm heavily involved in the China market; Douglas Paal, a former deputy secretary of state during the Clinton years who once suggested that Warren Christopher be fired because he was not accommodating enough towards Beijing; and, of course, the omnipresent Brent Scowcroft. Conference participants worried that the "images of the June 1989 killings around Tiananmen Square remain...vivid for most Americans," and predictably concluded that the U.S. "should promptly lift post-Tiananmen economic sanctions on China that have become counterproductive or place an unnecessary burden on U.S. business." A book produced by the Columbia conference was subsequently published.

Most offensive about the China lobby's campaign is its brazen dishonesty. The U.S.-China Business Council portrays in lurid detail the disaster that awaits if Beijing's MFN status were to be cut off. It predicts that such a "declaration of economic war" would lead to the explosion of the U.S. trade deficit and the layoff of tens of thousands of American workers as U.S. exports to China "drop almost to zero." The council further maintains that human rights improvements in China will come naturally as a result of increased trade.

Meanwhile, the annual U.S. trade deficit with China now tops $40 billion, even larger than the deficit with Japan, which previously held first place. The true concern of American business—which in 1995 exported more to Taiwan's 21 million people ($19 billion) than it did to China's 1.2 billion people (under $12 billion)—is not protecting American exports and jobs, but access to China's vast supply of cheap labor.

China's apologists argue that the United States has no leverage with Beijing, which, they say, will simply expand commerce with other nations if the United States makes too many demands on the human rights front. Yet the United States is not only China's largest trading partner but also its biggest source of investment and technology.

All of this gives the U.S. plenty of negotiating strength. Indeed, the Clinton administration has used such leverage to force China to make concessions on economic issues such as intellectual property rights and market access. "There's a clear double standard," says Jendrzjczyk of Human Rights Watch. "On human rights, the United States claims to be completely impotent but in other areas it's willing to make use of leverage it supposedly doesn't have."

The China lobby's money carries more weight than the force of its arguments, however. The primary obstacle it faces is public opinion, which remains extremely hostile to Beijing. Indeed, it's remarkable that opponents of MFN for China—little more than a few unions and environmental groups—have been able to wage such an effective battle in the face of the millionaire campaign being run by the Fortune 500. "The fact that they still haven't succeeded [in winning over public opinion] shows how strongly human rights concerns have resonated in this debate," says one Hill staffer from the anti-MFN camp. "If it weren't for that, we would have been squashed long ago."

CHAPTER FIVE

SEND LAWYERS, GUNS AND MONEY

Lobbying and the Merchants of Death

"I would feel more guilty selling sugar-coated breakfast cereal to kids than selling weapons to democratic nations."
—Arms lobbyist Joel Johnson,
who supports selling American weaponry
to "democratic" nations such as Saudi Arabia and Indonesia.

The foreign lobbyists discussed in the last chapter probably comprise the most ethically deranged sector of the lobbying industry, but the direct cost to taxpayers of their escapades is relatively paltry (foreign aid packages that generally amount to no more than a few hundred million dollars). Now you will meet a group whose rampages result in a far bigger hit on the federal treasury: lobbyists for the arms industry. The vast sums allocated each year to the Pentagon—$260 billion in 1997—constitutes the largest gravy train for private interests in the history of mankind.

The scale of the plunder is not the only reason that military lobbyists deserve special scrutiny. When the weapons industry convinces Congress to dole out money for more tanks and planes, a de facto outcome is that less money is left for social programs. The choice truly is between guns and butter.

Yet eight years after the Berlin Wall came down, the defense budget sits at the same level, in real dollars, as it did during the 1950s, the coldest days of the Cold War. It has declined only 23 percent from its all time peak under Ronald Reagan. As of 1997, the U.S. was spending almost as much on defense as the rest of the world combined—and internal Defense Department studies show a doubling of the Pentagon's budget over the next twenty years.

The money now being spent on "defense" is completely out of proportion to any credible threat to national security. The United States accounts for about half of all military spending on the planet and with the Soviet Union gone, the gravest "threat" to national security is posed by "rogue" nations such as North Korea, Libya, Iran and Iraq.

The absurdity of this situation is matched only by the absurdity of the military industry's post-Cold War lobbying efforts, which have been greatly increased in order to fend off any threat to its money pipeline. Here's an example of just how ridiculous things have become: A few years ago, it appeared that Congress might kill off a relic of the Cold War, the V-22 Osprey, a vertical lift-off plane whose prime contractors are Boeing and Bell Helicopter. From the perspective of Pentagon porkers and arms makers, the V-22 has special appeal: since it is incapable of carrying any of the military's current inventory of fighting vehicles, it has opened the door to a subsidiary boondoggle, the armored dune buggy. Said buggy, which is capable of attaining speeds of 80 miles per hour, is being designed especially to fit on the V-22.

To help save the plane, lobbyists for the V-22 dreamed up *Alyssa, Albert & the Magic Plane*, a cartoon book that was distributed to members of Congress. The comic book opens with little Alyssa playing in her backyard with Albert, a stuffed animal who springs to life. The pair dream of attending the 1996 Olympics in Atlanta but grow despondent upon concluding that they won't be able to get to the games by bicycle (too far), truck (no drivers license), boat (no water near Atlanta), the Space Shuttle (not practical), or a variety of other means.

Just as the cuddly duo have reached the point of despair a V-22—the "Magic Plane"—lands in the backyard to fly them to Atlanta. After "meeting people from all over the world and learning new games," Alyssa and Albert remember that "daddy would be done fixing the kitchen sink very soon and that they needed to get back home. Alyssa wished again for the Magic Plane to come take them home. And it did!"

The dramatic tale of Alyssa and other lobbying, combined with hefty campaign donations from Boeing and Bell, led Congress to save the V-22. Coming next: The arms makers sign up Barney the Dinosaur to lobby for Star Wars.

The Pentagon's Nightmare Scenario: Budget Cuts

Though the military budget remains in the stratosphere, life has become far more complicated for the arms lobby during the past decade. During the Cold War, the military-industrial complex needed only to point to the Soviet Union, and lawmakers would immediately sign over a check to cover yet another of the Pentagon's gold-plated boondoggles. With the Soviet Bear extinct and China and other future "threats" not yet on line, the public has grown somewhat more reluctant to tolerate Cold War levels of defense spending.

Hence, soon after the fall of the Berlin Wall the arms industry and the Pentagon began invoking the grave threat to national security posed by the "rogue" nations. But this strategy never galvanized the public. As Michael Klare has written in The Nation, "None of the prominent rogues have made any move in recent years to threaten U.S. interests seriously, and periodic claims of major breakthroughs by these states in acquiring nuclear or chemical weapons have rarely amounted to much....Only Iran now appears as a credible enemy...[but it] spends only about 1 percent of what the United States spends on defense [and its] poorly equipped military is a mere shadow of the force assembled by Saddam Hussein in 1990."

By 1997, the Pentagon had grown desperate to find a stand-in for the Red Army, as seen in a secret document prepared by the Air Force University that year and uncovered by journalist Andrew Cockburn. Peering into the second decade of the coming millennium, Air Force soothsayers were pointing to the emergence of a terrifying specter they called The Khan (as in Genghis). By this the "futurists" mean an aggressive China, enlarged by domination of the entire Korean Peninsula, not to mention Japan and possibly Vietnam. The Khan will be an economic superpower and thus able to develop and produce the most advanced forms of weaponry. It therefore follows that U.S. defense spending will have to rise commensurably to defend the West against this ominous Asian monster.

Elsewhere in the Pentagon officials are invoking the menace of "peer competitors," by which they mean China (though not yet grown to Khan dimensions) and, bizarrely, Russia. Yet others talk of GET, which stands for Generic Emerging Threat—a menace as yet undefined but against which the U.S. had better arm itself.

The Pet Rock Lobby

In addition to its failure to drum up a new "threat" to national security, the arms industry lobby is burdened by the shoddy nature of some of its wares. The primary cause here is that the chief mission of the U.S. defense industry is not to protect national security, but to inflate contractor profits.

This is seen in the case of McDonnell Douglas's hopeless C-17 cargo plane. Like many current Pentagon projects, the C-17 gained momentum following the 1979 Soviet invasion of Afghanistan, when the Carter administration pushed for a wave of new defense spending to counter the Red Menace. The Pentagon initially planned to buy 210 C-17s for $32 billion—$152 million apiece—but in 1990 cut the order to 120 planes for $36 billion—$333 million apiece. In 1993, the program was further reduced to 40 planes, with the per copy cost soaring to $700 million.

Since the original justification for the aircraft has vanished, the Pentagon and McDonnell Douglas now insist that the cargo plane is essential to national security because of its alleged ability to move personnel and tons of equipment to distant combat zones. Just as important is the C-17's much hyped capacity to land on short, dirt airstrips, and thus handle the dangerous task of re-supplying advance troops.

In reality, the C-17 is a threat to national security, and to anyone who is forced to ride it. A 1992 Congressional Research Service report detailed a few of the problems experienced by this monstrous boondoggle, including multiple problems with the software for the C-17's nineteen on-board computers. The C-17 also has a mysterious center-of-gravity problem, which makes take-off extremely dangerous unless the plane is fully loaded. When the aircraft is empty, sources say, Air Force crews keep two 7,950 pound cement blocs—known as the "pet rocks"—in the craft's forward area to ensure safe take-off. This means that the C-17 will either fly into action pre-loaded with nearly eight tons of cement or advance troops will be forced to tote along two "pet rocks" to load onto the plane after removing its cargo.

Even worse, the C-17 is incapable of carrying out its assigned task of forward re-supply. The enormous aircraft needs at least 4,000 feet of runway to land, 1,000 more than the Air Force claims. A former Pentagon official tells me that the C-17 cannot come down on a dirt airstrip because its jet engines will "ingest" earth. "You could land it on a concrete strip but if you try to put it down on dirt you'll end up with some very expensive repair bills," says this person, who points out that advance combat troops are not normally anywhere near a concrete landing strip.

This same person says that a used Boeing 747, which can be bought and modified for less than $100 million, can carry three times as much cargo as the C-17 and twice as far. In fact, the Pentagon's old twin engine C-123, which was used in Vietnam, could perform the C-17's job perfectly well. Unfortunately, the Pentagon hated that plane because it was inexpensive and lacked the glamour of a jet-engine aircraft. As the source points out, "this golden turkey represents a sizable chunk of the GNP and can be blown to smithereens by a $22 mortar shell."

In the Belly of the Beast

If the post-Cold War environment has left arms makers exposed, the industry still has plenty of assets when it comes to getting its way in Washington. Chief among them is that weapons makers, to an even greater extent than other industries, have especially tight links to the government bureaucracy. When the Pentagon in 1997 needed a team to prepare a report on "reshaping the U.S. military for the 21st century," it picked for the job a task force headed by Philip Odeen, president of BDM, one of the country's big defense companies. Odeen was ably assisted by other hacks for the weapons lobby, including Robert Riscassi, a former Army general who now serves as a vice president at Lockheed. The task force, known as the Quadrennial Defense Review, predictably concluded that force levels should be cut further, but the Pentagon's procurement budget should be increased, thereby ensuring future profits for the arms industry.

The Pentagon's Defense Policy Advisory Committee on Trade provides confidential recommendations to the Secretary of Defense on the sale of weapons abroad. Members have included CEOs from Lockheed, Boeing, Northrop Grumman and McDonnell, as well as a number of former Pentagon officials who now serve as consultants to the arms industry. Needless to say, the Advisory Committee invariably favors elimination of any barrier to foreign sales and the introduction of a host of new public subsidies to arms companies. Then there's the Pentagon's Defense Science Board, where Defense Department officials and industry executives join hands to lard out vast sums of money to fund research on future boondoggles. Past members at the science board have included former Defense Secretary William Perry; former CIA chief John Deutsch, and Paul Kaminski, the assistant secretary for defense.

Worthy of more detail is the Defense Trade Advisory Group (DTAG), the panel set up by the State Department to offer counsel in regard to the Direct Commercial Sales (DCS) program, by which defense contractors make private sales to foreign military and police forces. Details about the DCS program are hard to come by, since only deals worth more than $14 million must be reported to Congress. In theory, State allows the sale of weapons destined for a "defensive" role. It will not vend arms to an "aggressor" nation.

In practice, State authorizes sales to virtually any nation capable of paying for its purchases. Of some 20,000 requests for licenses made by vendors in 1994, State rejected just 209. During the Clinton years, State has sanctioned the sale of tank engines to Israel, trainer aircraft to Taiwan, and Black Hawk helicopters to Mexico. Also approved were deals with Guatemala, El Salvador, Colombia and Saudi Arabia.

None of this is surprising after examining the roster of DTAG, State's advisor on these deals. In 1995, 57 of the 60 panel members came from the arms industry. The group was headed at the time by William Schneider, a veteran of the military-industrial complex who served as undersecretary of state for security assistance during the Reagan/Bush years.

One especially enthusiastic DTAG member is Joel Johnson of the Aerospace Industries Association. Reflecting the judicious approach he brings to the committee, Johnson once told the *Los Angeles Times* that he "would feel more guilty selling sugar-coated breakfast cereal to kids" than he does about selling weapons abroad. After the Chinese government carried out its bloody crackdown at Tiananmen Square, Johnson fretted that the U.S. government might prevent arms companies from cutting new deals with Beijing. "If we get out of the Chinese market now, we could lose out on sales well into the next century," he told William Hartung, an analyst at the World Policy Institute. In any case, he added, Tiananmen was no big deal. "For the Chinese, whether it was 200 or 2,000 deaths, it's just a blip on the radar screen. It's like their version of Kent State."

The three non-industry members of DTAG are two lawyers and Janne Nolan, a polite centrist from the Brookings Institution. When former Arkansas Senator David Pryor questioned State Department officials about the objectivity of the group, they pointed to Nolan as providing balance.

DTAG is not a policy-making body, but it has lobbied the Clinton administration on proposals it reviews, such as revisions in export regulations and conventional arms transfer policy. "DTAG has frequent, high-level access to the people who are making policy," says Lora Lumpe of the Federation of American Scientists. "People from the arms control community are completely shut out of that loop."

Opening a New Front in the Lobbying Wars

The end of communism convinced the arms lobby that Congress could no longer be counted on to rubber stamp every new weapons program put in front of it by the military-industrial complex. Hence, many big defense firms greatly stepped up their beltway lobbying efforts following the fall of the Berlin Wall.

A first step taken by many companies was to move corporate offices to Washington, or to beef up existing D.C. operations. The rush to the beltway began in earnest in 1991, when

Grumman (later bought by Northrop, which in 1997 was purchased by Lockheed) moved from St. Louis to Falls Church in northern Virginia. As then-CEO William Anders told the *New York Times*, the move was made so as to bring the company's "leadership closer to our principal customers and policy makers." Other companies followed suit, including the nation's biggest defense contractor, Lockheed, which moved from Calbasas, California, to Bethesda, Maryland, after its merger with Martin Marietta in 1995. "There are no longer plenty of programs to go around," John Harbison, a vice president at Booz-Allen & Hamilton, told *Defense News* in 1996 in explaining the eastward march.

The arms makers dramatically increased their spending on lobbying programs as well. In 1987, GE was considered to be the defense industry's lobbying powerhouse, with 19 lobbyists working in Washington. Raytheon, Hughes and United Technology didn't have a single influence peddler registered with Congress. Lobbying expenditures by the big defense firms averaged about $40,000 per year. As late as 1991, the ten biggest defense companies had a total of 108 lobbyists registered in Washington.

As of mid-1997, Lockheed Martin alone has 87 lobbyists registered with Congress, 26 working out of the company's own offices and 61 at outside firms that the company had on retainer. Lockheed's total lobbying expenditures for 1996 totaled $3.8 million, 10 times more than the combined lobbying expenditures for the ten biggest defense contractors in 1985.

While Boeing has fewer lobbyists on its payroll—70—it spent more than Lockheed, shelling out $5.2 million for lobbying in 1996. Other arms makers have similarly huge efforts, with Northrop employing 58 lobbyists and McDonnell Douglas 53.

The merchants of death have also stepped up their pace of campaign contributions. In 1987, political contributions by weapons companies averaged a few hundred thousand dollars a year. In 1996, Lockheed Martin ponied up $2.3 million in PAC and soft money contributions to the big parties. All told, defense makers delivered more than $11 million to friends in high places during the 1996 presidential and congressional campaigns.

To build further political support on Capitol Hill, arms makers have begun promoting weapons systems as being not only vital to national security but jobs programs to boot. To make the jobs pitch work, defense makers spread out contracts and subcontracts across the nation, thereby giving every state—and more importantly, most members of Congress—a stake in a given arms program.

Rockwell made especially smart use of this tactic in lobbying for its B-1 bomber, the hideously expensive plane deemed so unreliable that the Air Force didn't dare send it into combat during the Gulf War (and now put out to pasture with the National Guard, which will presumably use the craft to conduct urgent national security tasks such as bombing marijuana plantations). Some 5,000 companies in all 48 contiguous states worked on the B-1. The wings were made in Nashville, the tail assembly in Baltimore, engines near Cincinnati, wheels in Akron and electronic units in Nashua, New Hampshire. "From the standpoint of efficiency, to try to make a [weapons system] in as many congressional districts as possible is nuts," former Rep. Patricia Schroeder told the *New York Times* a few years back. "But from a lobbying standpoint it's incredibly sophisticated."

An Army of Lobbyists:
The Pentagon's Job Placement Program

The arms lobby's firepower is further augmented by the nonstop revolving door between the Pentagon and the defense industry. Common Cause published a study some years ago which showed that between 1983 and 1985, 3,745 officers with the rank of major or above, along with top level civilian employees at the Pentagon, had gone to work for arms contractors. The revolving door is spinning just as fast today, with thousands of Cold War veterans—both bureaucrats and soldiers—now serving as consultants and lobbyists to the arms industry, as well as on the boards of directors of the big weapons makers.

Until 1997, Lockheed was headed by Norman Augustine, a former secretary of the army. The company's board includes retired Gen. Riscassi, mentioned above as a member of the Pentagon panel that issued a report on future defense priorities. Among the top lobbyists at the company's corporate offices in Bethesda, Maryland, are Alan Ptak, a former Navy deputy secretary of defense, and Jack Overstreet, ex-chief of weapons systems at the Air Force.

Then there's SAIC, a huge high-tech firm, which receives more contracts from the government than any other company. It translates and decodes intercepts for the NSA, provides the CIA with computer software to analyze intelligence data, and has a variety of contracts working on the Star Wars missile defense program. SAIC's board members have included two former defense secretaries—William Perry and Melvin Laird—and three former heads of the CIA—John Deutsch, Bobby Ray Inman, and Robert Gates. Most top positions at the firm are filled by retired military officials, spooks, former Congressional staffers and employees of federal agencies

In the years immediately following World War II, military officers did not commonly go to work for defense companies upon retiring from active duty (with the exception of the Air Force, which has always been the most corrupt service branch). There was a social stigma about using influence and knowledge attained while serving one's country as tools of profiteering. Today, such inhibitions have all but disappeared.

Ernie Fitzgerald is the Air Force official who was fired by
President Nixon because he blew the whistle on cost overruns
on Lockheed's C-130. Fitzgerald sued to get his job back and
was reinstated four years later following a long court battle.
Fitzgerald is still at the Pentagon and is as crotchety as ever
about the corruption there. Here's how he explains the inner
workings of the revolving door:

Military officers for the most part are forced to retire when
their family expenses are at a peak—they've got a couple of
kids in college and they're still paying a mortgage. They won't
starve on their retired pay. But at the same time they can't
keep up their lifestyle. What happens in our system is that the
services see one of their management duties as placing their
retired officers, just like a good university will place its gradu-
ates. And the place the services have the most influence at is
with the contractors.

If you're a good clean-living officer and you don't get drunk at
lunch or get caught messing around with the opposite sex in
the office, and you don't raise too much of a fuss about horror
stories you come across—when you retire, a nice man will
come calling. Typically he'll be another retired officer. And
he'll be driving a fancy car, a Mercedes or equivalent, and
wearing a $2,000 suit and Gucci shoes and Rolex watch. He
will offer to make a comfortable life for you by getting you a
comfortable job at one of the contractors.

Now, if you go around kicking people in the shins, raising hell
about the outrages committed by the big contractors, no nice
man comes calling. It's that simple.

Sell, Sell, Sell: Lobbyists and Foreign Arms Sales

A particularly illuminating case of the revolving door in
action is that of retired Lt. Gen. Howard Fish. A former
Pentagon staffer I interviewed says Fish worked in the
Pentagon for decades but always as a staff officer. "He never

commanded anything in his life," this person says. "He was one of the all-time champions of service in the Pentagon, always holding ass-kissing positions."

During the Nixon and Ford administrations, Fish headed the Defense Security Assistance Agency (DSAA), the Pentagon bureau that handles foreign military sales and one of the more corrupt components of the military establishment. The DSAA has a field staff of about 1,000 people who work out of the U.S. embassy in some 75 countries. They offer everything from briefings on weapons systems to demonstrations of major aircraft, in addition to arranging the financing needed to close a deal.

The DSAA receives a 3 percent commission per sale—which provides about 80 percent of its operating budget—and agency personnel are promoted on the basis of their ability to move weaponry. Due to this dynamic, says a 1991 report from Congress's now defunct Office of Technology Assessment, "there is powerful incentive for DSAA personnel to make as many sales as possible."

As head of the DSAA, Fish was an exuberant promoter of selling weapons to any and all buyers. According to William Hartung of the World Policy Institute, Fish played a key role in watering down the Arms Export Control Act of 1976, which would have placed a ceiling on total foreign arms sales and given Congress the right to veto sales on human rights grounds.

During the early 1970s, Fish was among several officials who were found to have passed sensitive information about contractual matters to several big arms makers, including Lockheed and LTV Aerospace & Defense. The information was of great use to the arms makers, as it involved plans for overseas sales and information about what weapons systems might be targeted for cuts. The affair caused a huge scandal inside the Pentagon, but Fish escaped censure.

At roughly the same time Fish became heavily involved in sales to Iran, then headed by the Shah. Iran was seen as an enormous cash cow for the Pentagon and the arms makers. The environment surrounding the arms trade was so corrupt that even the Shah became incensed, especially about American "brokers" for U.S. companies who were running around Iran and receiving huge commissions on deals they arranged. When the Shah sought to eliminate bribes and fees paid to these brokers, Fish fought him every inch of the way, claiming that this would impinge on the flexibility contractors needed to close deals.

Later in the decade Fish began to take a keen interest in Egypt, as that nation was coming on-line as a major buyer of U.S. weaponry. As a result of the 1978 Camp David accords, Egypt was to receive $1 billion per year in military aid. To ship weapons to the Egyptians, the Pentagon signed an exclusive contract with a company called Eatsco, which was formed by an Egyptian government official named Hussein K. Salem and a retired CIA official named Thomas Clines, who later played a prominent role in the Iran-Contra scandal. A third principal, though a silent one, was Edwin Wilson, the retired CIA agent who at the time was living in Libya and providing military equipment and training to the government of Muammar Quaddafi. Wilson is currently serving a 52-year prison term for arranging shipments of explosives to Quaddafi, and for subsequent attempts to kill witnesses against him.

It later turned out that Eatsco had overbilled the Pentagon by $8 million on shipments to the Egyptians. In one case, Eatsco billed the government $1.3 million for a shipment that cost about half that much. The mark-up increased further on a $46,409 shipment for which Eatsco billed the government $210,904.

It also turned out that Eatsco had two additional principals, both silent partners who worked inside the government. The two were Fish's closest cronies at the Pentagon, Richard Secord, later another big player in the Iran-Contra affair, and Erich von Marbod, who served as Fish's second in command at the DSAA. Secord and von Marbod were forced to retire from the Pentagon as a result of the Eatsco affair, though the cause was hushed up.

Fish's work at the Pentagon provided him with the perfect resume when he decided to retire from government in the late 1970s. He quickly found work with LTV—one of the two firms he had provided classified information to a few years earlier. Within months of his resignation he turned up in Malaysia, where he was hawking A-7 fighters. Fish also hired von Marbod to work at LTV's Paris offices.

Fish later worked as the head of international marketing for Loral, another big weapons maker, and then took charge of the American League for Exports and Security Assistance (ALESA) in the late 1980s. The latter outfit is one of the many powerful trade groups formed by arms makers—others include the Aerospace Industries Association and the American Defense Preparedness Association—to lobby for higher military outlays at home and greater U.S. military involvement abroad.

One of Fish's chief missions has been promoting the sale of weapons to the Middle East, especially to Saudi Arabia where Fish has intimate connections (he kept a picture of Saudi King Fahd on a bookcase at his office). Back in 1989, Fish met with chief of staff John Sununu and National Security Advisor Brent Scowcroft in a successful effort to convince the Bush administration to sell front-line tanks and supersonic fighters to Arab countries.

An impressive display of the ALESA's efforts came in the early 1990s, when at the behest of weapons makers it helped form the Middle East Action Group to press for deals then in the pipeline with the Saudis. Other members of the coalition included GE, Ford, Bechtel, Boeing, and the U.S.-Arab Chamber of Commerce

In addition to Fish, the Action Group also retained the services of a number of high-powered consultants with links to the Saudis. These include:

- Dov Zakheim, a former deputy defense undersecretary for Reagan, chief defense adviser to Bob Dole during the 1996 presidential campaign and head of a consulting firm called SPC International. Zakheim is an ordained rabbi with close ties to the American Jewish community. His great credibility with the pro-Israel lobby makes Zakheim especially useful to arms makers lobbying for sales to Arab countries.

- Sandra Charles served on the National Security Council as director for Middle East Affairs during the Bush years. After retiring, she formed a consulting firm, C&O Resources, which handles foreign policy analysis, business development, and arms sales to the Middle East, including Saudi Arabia.

- Robert Lilac, head of Lilac Associates, which represents both arms contractors and foreign governments who buy weapons from U.S. companies. Lilac is a former Air Force officer who also served on the National Security Council during the Reagan years, where he was an intimate companion with several key figures in the Iran-Contra scandal, especially Richard Secord. Lilac commands a premium among the weapons makers due to his close relationship with Prince Bandar, the long-time Saudi ambassador to the U.S., who Lilac worked for immediately after he left government service. As Joel Johnson of Aerospace Industries Association once explained, "Bob knows the Saudi system, he knows the industry, and he knows the Pentagon."

The Middle East Working Group's lobbying campaign was laid out in a 300-page strategy book. It shows that the coalition assigned individuals to work with the White House, the State Department, the National Security Council, the Pentagon, key committees of Congress, the media, think tanks, veterans groups and patriotic organizations. The strategy book also called for member companies to mobilize their workers, middle managers and executives to flood Washington with telegrams and phone calls supporting arms sales.

Another group focused on putting the best possible spin on arms sales. Among the themes developed for public consumption were that "the sooner we bolster the Saudi military, the sooner...[U.S. military personnel in Saudi Arabia] will be able to return to the United States" and that "blocking arms sales...is a sure way to cripple our economy and cause unnecessary layoffs of thousands of professionals." The coalition didn't get everything it asked for, but its member companies succeeded in ramming billions of dollars of dollars worth of deals through Congress during the past few years.

Fish recently left the league to become a consultant to Lockheed Martin. He also wears a second hat as a member of the export policy subcommittee of the DPACT, where he advises the Pentagon on the international arms trade.

The Invisible Man

It's not only Pentagon retirees who moving through the revolving door to work for the defense industry. Countless former denizens of Capitol Hill also make the move, lured by the big bucks offered up by weapons makers. Paul Magliocchetti left a job at the House Appropriations Committee in 1988 and now heads a powerful lobby shop that caters to defense firms. In a 1996 report, *Legal Times* called Magliocchetti "The Invisible Man," and detailed how an "obscure Hill aide...became a million dollar lobbyist."

Magliocchetti's specialty when he worked on the Hill was

defense appropriations. Before that he worked at the General Accounting Office, where he conducted audits and investigations of the Pentagon. All this helped Magliocchetti learn the nuts and bolts of the defense industry and the budget process, two skills that proved vital when he decided to strike out on his own as a lobbyist. *Legal Times* quoted former Rep. Charles Wilson as saying, "The thing about Paul is [he and his lobbying aides] just always had such a wealth of knowledge, and they could really make their case...They just knew [in] what line of the bill" they should place a special favor to their clients.

Magliocchetti incorporated his lobbying firm in October of 1988. He was still drawing a salary at the House until at least two months later. Within months of retiring he had signed up his first client, the Sikorsky Aircraft Division of United Technologies.

Many of Magliocchetti's current aides previously worked at the Pentagon, including Thomas Veltri, who had served as the Air Force's liaison with Appropriations Committees in Congress. Magliocchetti's firm also runs a generous political action committee—it gave more than $75,000 during the 1996 election cycle—and throws an annual Christmas party for members of Congress and their staffers at the Alpine restaurant in Arlington, just across the Potomac from Washington.

All of this has paid off nicely. Magliocchetti, who was forced to eke out a modest living on his $65,200-a-year salary at House Appropriations, now rakes in big fees from dozens of firms. *Legal Times* says his company's revenues topped $1 million during the first half of 1996, ranking it 42nd on the newspaper's ranking of top lobby shop money earners.

Government Issue Golden Parachutes

Stepped up lobbying efforts by the arms industry have paid big dividends these past few years. Even as Congress hacks away at social programs, it has granted virtually every budgetary wish of the defense lords.

Norman Augustine of Lockheed: From the hapless F-22 fighter to government subsidies for weapons makers, this man has probably lifted more money from your pocket than anyone else in America.

One especially egregious assault on the federal treasury involves a Pentagon decision to reimburse defense contractors for expenses related to mergers and acquisitions. This taxpayer rip-off dates to June 3, 1993. On that day, the CEOs of Martin Marietta, GM Hughes Electronics, Lockheed and Loral Corporation wrote a letter to then Under Secretary of Defense John Deutsch saying that the Pentagon's policy at that time of refusing to help pay for merger costs would "discourage needed restructuring...[and] undermine the defense industrial base."

Deutsch responded swiftly. Just a month later, he unilaterally overruled the Pentagon's own internal auditors and decreed that henceforth contractors could submit merger-related bills to the Defense Department for review.

That the top Pentagon brass was so sensitive to the CEOs, who were led by Norman Augustine of Martin Marietta, was understandable. Before moving to the Pentagon, Deutsch had served as a consultant to Augustine's firm for nine years, earning $425,000. Then Defense Secretary William Perry was part owner of a firm, Technology Strategies & Alliances, which had a contract with Martin Marietta until 1992.

Recognizing that the public might not look kindly upon the new policy, Deutsch and the Pentagon prudently failed to notify Congress of the payoff plan. The program only came to light in early 1994, when former Senator Sam Nunn, who then headed the Senate Armed Services Committee, received a memo showing that Martin Marietta was seeking $60 million from the Pentagon to help pay for its $208 million acquisition of General Dynamic's space division. The Pentagon didn't even publish the decision in the Federal Register until months after it was made.

That $60 million request from Martin Marietta foreshadowed a stampede by big defense contractors heading for the public trough. Lockheed and Martin Marietta merged in March 1995, a move that will eliminate 30,000 jobs. The new company, Lockheed Martin, later submitted bills to the federal government for more than $1 billion in restructuring costs. The bills included a plea for taxpayer help in paying for $31 million out of $92 million in bonuses that the companies paid to their top executives in the merger's aftermath. Augustine, who became CEO of the new company, was showered with a cash payment of $10.6 million, as well as stock options worth $9.5 million. Daniel Tellep, who had been president of Lockheed, pocketed the same amount in stock options as well as $4.3 million in cash. (The Pentagon gave preliminary approval for $16 million of the bonus money requested and is reviewing the rest.)

Ten months after Lockheed Martin was formed, the new

company swallowed up the Loral Corporation. After agreeing to sell his firm, Loral's CEO Bernard Schwartz—who was one of the letter writers to Deutsch—received a $35 million bonus, part of which taxpayers were also asked to cover.

Other defense contractors have moved to cash in on the Pentagon's largesse. By 1997, the government was reviewing 30 applications for merger subsidies totaling $2 billion.

The weapons makers and the Pentagon insist that post-Cold War cuts in military spending have made industry consolidation necessary. Further, they claim, mergers will lead to greater efficiency and therefore reduce the prices defense companies charge the government. "I'm puzzled at how a policy that saves the government billions of dollars can be termed a subsidy," Chip Manor, a Lockheed spokesman, told me when I asked about the Pentagon policy.

Yet it is far from clear that the savings promised by the arms industry will ever materialize. A 1996 report from the Government Accounting Office examined eight defense mergers that had been approved by the Pentagon and found that actual savings realized are less than half of what defense companies had estimated when applying for subsidies.

We Arm the World

To ensure that they remain profitable in the event, however unlikely, that Congress should decide to cut the domestic defense budget, arms makers have aggressively lobbied for greater foreign sales. Between 1993 and 1996, the government approved about $75 billion worth of arms exports, to 160 of the world's 180 nations (about half of all sales went to non-democratic countries). The U.S. controls more than half of the international arms market, and foreign purchases now account for about 25 percent of all defense orders, up from 15 percent in the 1980s.

It's hard to see how exporting weapons can possibly enhance U.S. or international security. A large share of

American exports go to countries at war and soon end up on the battlefield. U.S. troops based abroad are also endangered by American exports. As a CIA report from 1995 noted, "the acquisition of advanced conventional weapons and technologies by hostile countries could result in significant casualties being inflicted on U.S. forced or regional allies." In fact, U.S. troops deployed to Bosnia, Haiti, Somalia, Kuwait and Panama have confronted foreign forces armed with weapons that were made in America.

None of this has stopped the government from increasing federal subsidies for arms exports—which total more than $7.5 billion annually at the behest of the weapons lobby. In September of 1996, President Clinton agreed to eliminate "recoupment fees," this being a special tax on foreign military sales that allowed the federal treasury to recover a portion of taxpayer-funded R&D costs. Two months later, the Pentagon inaugurated its new "Defense Export Loan Guarantee" program by which the government will underwrite the sale of U.S. weapons to a selected list of 38 foreign countries. If purchasers default, taxpayers will pick up the bill.

In early 1997, the administration again caved to the weapons makers. This time it lifted a ban on the sale of advanced weaponry—for example, fighter jets and missiles—to South America, which had been imposed during the Carter years when the continent was largely ruled by military regimes.

The last thing Latin America needs is an arms race to acquire a new generation of high-priced weaponry. Most Latin American nations have only recently emerged from long periods of military rule and the armed forces remain politically powerful. Furthermore, Latin governments are smothering in debt and have little money available to pay for social programs, let alone F-16s.

Needless to say, the arms industry is not terribly interested in such issues. Since sales of fighter planes are the companies' biggest money maker, they rallied as one in seeking to overturn the 25-year old ban. The effort was particularly intense because traditional big volume buyers in the Middle East are uniformly cash-strapped, leaving the arms makers desperate to crack new markets.

Until 1994, the Clinton administration indicated it favored maintenance of the Latin arms embargo. That year it prevented Lockheed from attending an international air show in Chile. The arms lobby was   outraged, particularly as Britain, France, Israel, Russia and vendors from at least two dozen other companies used the show to hawk their wares.

The Clinton administration was not the only obstacle in the arms makers' path. For if the supply was willing, the demand was not. Latin nations had not expressed any real interest in buying advanced weaponry, least of all the fighter planes the arms makers were so keen to off-load. In 1982, Venezuela had received a waiver from the Reagan administration that allowed it to buy 26 F-16s, but the country did not have the money to fly or maintain the planes. Most simply sat parked in Air Force hangars.

To start the ball rolling on the supply side, DPACT issued a study in 1995 calling for a "balanced policy" that would allow South American nations to meet "the demands...for needed equipment modernization." Joel Johnson, who chaired the panel, later said that the U.S. was "treat[ing] the Latins like children when we say they can't have new planes."

During the 1996 campaign, the arms lobby got the GOP to include a plank in its platform promising that the Clinton administration's "policy of denying most Latin American countries the opportunity to replace their obsolescent military equipment...will be reversed by a Republican administration." That same year, more than 100 members of Congress signed two separate letters to the Clinton administration—drafted by the merchants of death themselves—claiming that the Latin ban had cost U.S. companies $4 billion in exports and 40,000 jobs.

The arms lobby also moved to sweep away demand side barriers. As *Time* magazine reported, the Pentagon in March of 1996 sent advanced fighters to Chile for an air show. The Defense Department also arranged for Puerto Rican National Guard pilots to fly Brazilian generals in F-16s. Within months, Brazil and Chile—whose military is less pressed for cash than most of its neighbors as it receives 10 percent of national copper exports—had taken the bait, with both nations contacting the Pentagon to inquire about possible sales.

The rest was simple. When William Perry resigned as Secretary of Defense in 1997 he wrote a letter to Clinton urging him to reconsider the ban. Perry's successor, William Cohen, also began lobbying for the change shortly after he joined the administration. The spring of 1997 saw Clinton's inevitable capitulation, with the president unveiling a draft policy on arms sales to South America that was virtually identical to the one proposed by DPACT in its original 1995 report.

Pork Central: The Appropriations Trough

Some of the fiercest military lobbying battles have involved fights to obtain (or maintain) appropriations for new weapons programs. This is where the real pork lies, as any first generation system costs billions and billions of dollars. A really good contract will allow a contractor to plunder the federal treasury for decades, from R&D through final sales and then post-production business, such as maintenance and repairs, and modifications.

One costly taxpayer swindle involves Lockheed's F-22 fighter, a plane originally conceived as a counter to a new generation of Soviet fighters and planned to be based at European air bases in order to deter a Warsaw Pact assault on NATO forces. Since this function no longer serves as an alibi, Lockheed's

promo material for the F-22 now argues that the plane is needed because of the threat posed by "regional aggressors," pointing here to the formidable aircraft possessed by potential U.S.
adversaries. Yet according to *Harper's*, if a single nation somehow gained control of every Soviet MIG-29 and Su-27 on the
planet, the U.S. Air Force already has a tactical fleet that
would outnumber this ominous threat by seven to one. A
Congressional Budget Office report in 1995 said that "the F-22
may provide more capability to attack enemy fighters than the
United States needs." A GAO report the following year concluded that "the aircraft and air defense forces of potential
adversaries have not been substantially improved and do not
pose a serious threat."

Like all big-money weapons projects, the F-22 has suffered
outrageous cost overruns. The Pentagon initially estimated
that the plane would cost $60 million each, a price that has
now risen to $148 million each. Lockheed succeeded in dri-
ving up the cost by covering the plane with as much high-tech
gold-plating as it could dream up—"every extra except fuzzy
dice," *Harper's* said. All the additional hardware added 12,000
pounds to the plane's weight, making it impossible for the
fighter to carry out one of its supposed strong suits—flying at
supersonic speeds—other than for brief bursts.

Despite all of its drawbacks, Lockheed has succeeded in
maintaining hefty funding for the plane (though the initial
order of 438 has been reduced to 339). In a bid to ensure
Congressional support, the company lavished out portions of
the F-22 pie to 676 companies in 44 states. In 1990, Lockheed
had the foresight to move the main F-22 production plant to
Georgia, home of then Senate Armed Services chairman Sam
Nunn, widely known during his years of public service as the
"Senator from Lockheed." After Nunn retired, another
Georgian, House Speaker Newt Gingrich, stepped in to lead
Congressional forces battling for the F-22.

The boldest move by Lockheed lobbyists came in the early-1990s, when even a few defense hawks were getting squeamish about the F-22's soaring costs and dwindling promise. The company then began circulating promo literature that laid out the top threats to American air supremacy, a list that includes everything from Russian MIG-29s owned by nations such as Iraq and North Korea to Lockheed's own F-16s, which the company has sold to "hostile" nations like Israel, South Korea and Canada. Lockheed goes so far as to boast that the F-22 can stymie the air defense radar systems which it has installed on the planes it has previously exported abroad. "We can't predict the future 30 years from now," Jeff Rhodes, a Lockheed spokesman, said in an interview. "A military dictator could take power in a country [that owns Lockheed aircraft] which is currently an ally."

With amazing audacity, Lockheed and the Pentagon are already stating that the F-22 might be made available to foreign countries as a means of reducing per unit costs. Possible buyers are Japan, Israel and Saudi Arabia. Already, one can hear Lockheed's next battle cry: Give us money to develop a new plane that can counter the dread threat posed by foreign nations which own the F-22!

The Mother of All Boondoggles

A full listing of Pentagon boondoggles would require a multi-volume collection. However, there is one project that stands out as perhaps the most egregious taxpayer rip-off of the post World War II period: The B-2 bomber, whose stealth technology is supposed to make it invisible to enemy radar.

The B-2 is the single most expensive piece of military equipment ever designed, costing three times its weight in gold and carrying a per unit price of about $2 billion. Congress has already allocated $44 billion for the project, a figure that exceeds the annual defense budget for all but a few nations in the world.

When Northrop-Grumman, the plane's prime contractor, was awarded the B-2 contract by the Reagan administration in 1981, the company and the Pentagon sold it as a remarkable new weapon which could penetrate deep into Soviet air space, inflict heavy damage and then safely fly home. Northrop executives were alarmed after Mikhail Gorbachev took power and began dismantling the communist system. An internal company memo from the period suggested that Northrop should begin selling the B-2 as "a prudent hedge against the uncertainty that [Gorbachev] may fail (or change his mind)."

Northrop was forced to come up with a new PR spin when Gorbachev was evicted from power and Boris Yeltsin decreed the end of the Soviet Union. The company has since claimed (among other things) that as the number of forward-deployed aircraft carriers declines and the U.S. gradually withdraws from its overseas bases, the B-2 will become more vital than ever because of its ability to carry out long-range missions from bases in the U.S.

Whatever the spin, Northrop's fundamental problem is that its plane is a dog. The B-2 employs a technology—stealth—that has never been shown to work. A Pentagon source who has reviewed classified data calls stealth "the biggest fraud ever perpetrated on the American public." He says that during the Gulf War, British destroyers picked up stealth crafts from 40 miles away. U.S. radar identified them at up to five times that distance. In regard to the B-2 specifically, this source points out that the bomber weighs a staggering 360,000 pounds. "There's no way to hide something like that," he states, adding that the B-2's gigantic size makes it "stick out like a dog turd in a fish bowl."

The conventional wisdom is that stealth craft, especially the F-117, played a central role in the Gulf War. In fact, stealth was completely irrelevant. The key to the Allied victory was that the Iraqi army suffered the largest mass desertions in histo-

© Jim Levitt, Impact Visuals

By stealth: The B-2 is the single most expensive piece of military equipment ever designed, costing three times its weight in gold and carrying a per unit price of about $2 billion.

ry; up to 175,000 soldiers fled the front before the ground combat began. The desertions resulted from Saddam Hussein's having stuffed the front with segregated units of Shiite and Kurd troops. Realizing that they were merely cannon fodder, huge numbers returned to their villages. That left some 25,000 troops to confront 400,000 U.S.-led soldiers. The latter could have walked in with swords.

Even if stealth technology worked, the B-2 wouldn't. The plane's stealth coating is extremely frail and suffers serious damage if exposed to rain or sun. The plane needs to be recoated frequently and B-2 pilots are only allowed to fly the bomber for a few hours per week. A 1997 General Accounting Office report said that "it is unlikely that the aircraft's sensitivity to moisture and climates or the need for controlled environments to fix low-observability problems will ever be fully resolved, even with improved materials and repair processes."

Stealth technology is just the start of the B-2's problems. Another GAO report, this one from 1995, found that the bomber's radar system malfunctions, leaving the plane unable to distinguish between a mountain and a rain cloud. The same GAO report concluded, "After 14 years of development... including six years of flight testing, the Air Force has yet to demonstrate that the B-2 design will meet some of its most important mission requirements."

A sign of the B-2's troubles came in the spring of 1997. Though the bomber had already performed substantial test flights, it was only on April 1 of that year that it was certified as combat ready and put on active duty. Northrop immediately announced in a series of newspaper ads that with the bomber finally fit for action, America's enemies had better watch their step. Within days, a shaft assembly in one of the engines of one of the planes cracked and the B-2 was withdrawn from the active roster.

Dracula's Revenge

There is a general recognition that the B-2 is a grotesque boondoggle. Already back in 1989, the *Washington Post* was reporting that consensus on the need for the B-2 had "crumbled," and was predicting its imminent demise. The original order for the plane shrank from 132 to 75 and then, in 1992, Congress and President Bush agreed to a compromise that terminated the program with an order of 20 planes. Several Pentagon reports have concluded that there is no need to build any more of the bombers and the Air Force itself has said it can't afford the plane, preferring to spend its money instead on short-range tactical jets it can base overseas.

Despite all of this, Northrop and its allies have scored a series of major victories these past few years. In 1995, Northrop got Congress to approve $493 million in new money for the bomber. During the presidential campaign the following year, Clinton, playing to voters in California—where Northrop and the B-2 production lines are located—added one more bomber to the package. In 1997, hawks in Congress led by Rep. Norm Dicks of Washington state, home to Boeing, a key subcontractor on the B-2, began pressing to raise the order back up to 30.

Why does the B-2 live on? The answer can be found in the expensive and multi-pronged lobbying campaign Northrop has conducted over most of the past decade. That campaign well illustrates why Congress continues to approve Cold War-era military budgets despite there being no plausible threat to the nation's security.

Northrop's lobbying for the B-2 has covered all of the bases, from hiring up former Pentagon officials to press Congress, to orchestrating fake "grassroots" uprisings. The company's top in-house lobbyist on the B-2 is Robert Helm, a former Pentagon Comptroller. He joined the company in 1994, replacing Togo West, who had been named secretary of the army. Offering outside counsel is Michael Balzano, a Nixon administration veteran who moved to the American Enterprise Institute and later worked on the Reagan/Bush campaign of 1980. Balzano now heads his own lobbying firm and represents almost all major defense contractors.

To provide further firepower on Capitol Hill, Northrop wheeled out Chuck Horner, the Air Force official who designed the Gulf War air campaign and who is revered by members of Congress. Horner, who is on Northrop's payroll, has testified several times before Congress about the B-2's awesome capabilities. The B-2 campaign has been further assisted by a number of other retired Pentagon officials. In 1995, former Air Force Secretary Don Rice was brought in to brief

Togo West: One of the arms makers' many agents inside government. Went from lobbying for the B-2 for Northrup-Grumman to a post as Secretary of the Army. Later named to head Veterans Affairs by Clinton.

wavering members on the day of the vote.

Northrop has greatly assisted the B-2's cause by doling out billions of dollars' worth of work to subcontractors across the country. As a result, the plane has been built, at various times, in 46 states and 383 congressional districts. Fourteen suppliers build the airframe and 25 firms make the electronic systems. Boeing received a subcontract for landing gear assemblies and then further subcontracted with at least ten more firms, ranging from giants such as Allied Signal and Goodyear to small companies such as Crissair of California and Cleveland Pneumatic. In short, there's a bit of pork for everybody, whether it's the $791 million in contracts spread across Texas or the $100,000 for West Virginia, where IMO Industries in Huntington makes clamps for the bomber.

Northrop relies on its vast network of subcontractors when it comes time to lobby for the plane's survival. During a crucial vote in 1995, Northrop brought together hundreds of subcontractor CEOs, who fanned out across the Capitol to press home state lawmakers.

Nor has Northrop skimped when it came to larding out campaign contributions to members of Congress. During the 1996 election cycle, the company poured more than $700,000 into political campaigns. About $80,000 of that was dispensed in June, the month that the House voted—by a margin of 213 to 210—to provide additional money for the B-2. Northrop's 213 allies received an average of $2,073 in PAC money from the company in 1996, while B-2 opponents received an average of a mere $113.

No member of Congress has shilled for the B-2 with greater fervor than Rep. Norm Dicks of Washington, who took in $10,000 from Northrop, the maximum allowed, during the 1995-1996 election cycle. Dicks even took advantage of the 1996 incident, in which Scott O'Grady was shot down during a reconnaissance flight in Bosnia, to seek support for his pet bomber. In several public statements, Dicks claimed that if the B-2 had been in America's arsenal at the time, this tragic event might not have taken place—as if the Air Force would ever dispatch and risk losing a $2 billion plane to conduct a simple reconnaissance mission. (When he was in the Senate in 1989, Defense Secretary William Cohen remarked that using the B-2 in any conventional war would be like sending "a Rolls-Royce down into a combat zone to pick up groceries.")

Northrop has arranged to fly lawmakers less enthusiastic than Dicks to visit its production lines in Pico Rivera and Palmdale, California. "I have visited the B-2 factory in

California, seen the B-2, climbed on its extraordinary wing, and in the cockpit, and met with representatives of the literally hundreds of firms that designed and built it," Rep. Sam Brownback marveled during House debate after returning from his tour. For black lawmakers, Northrop provides a list of minority-owned firms that have received work on the bomber, while women lawmakers get a list detailing all the female-owned firms taking part.

Similar efforts have been made to woo the public. To fine tune the PR spin for the B-2, Northrop once hired Democratic pollster Peter Hart, whose focus groups responded best to the theme that the bomber exposes fewer pilots to danger. The company has unleashed numerous advertising blitzes to take that message to the masses.

Northrop has twice retained that king of the "grassroots," Jack Bonner, to build public momentum for the B-2. In the early 1990s, when it appeared that the Cold War's end would lead to a collapse of congressional support for the B-2, Bonner's phoners helped turn the tide by prodding hundreds of organizations—representing seniors, minorities, religious groups, police chiefs, farmers and Rotary Club presidents—to send postcards to congress that called for continued production of the bomber.

In 1996, Northrop again hired Bonner after President Clinton decided to include no new money for the B-2 in the 1997 budget. Bonner & Associates sent a letter to Northrop employees and suppliers saying it was "absolutely vital" to inform President Clinton that his action would have a devastating impact "on you, on California, and on the country." The letter provided a toll-free number to call, with operators standing by to take orders for telegrams to the White House. Though Northrop and Bonner did not succeed in freeing up more cash for the B-2, Clinton and Congress maintained funding for the bombers that had been previously ordered.

Public opinion has also been targeted by a number of prominent defense intellectuals. The foremost public proponent of the B-2 is Loren Thompson of the Alexis de Tocqueville Institution in Arlington, an outfit that receives funding from Northrop. Thompson produces a steady stream of pro-B-2 op-ed articles and is regularly quoted in the press. He also is a regular witness before Congressional panels, telling one committee in 1997 that the B-2 is a miracle plane that can "fly anywhere in the world within a few hours, safely penetrate modern air defenses and precisely destroy up to 16 separate targets with minimum collateral damage." Such assurances were given despite the fact that at the time the B-2 had never even been certified as combat ready and had yet to fly a single mission.

Thompson also put together a letter from seven former secretaries of defense—Melvin Laird, James Schlesinger, Donald Rumsfield, Harold Brown, Caspar Weinberger, Frank Carlucci and Dick Cheney—in support of the B-2, which was used to great effect on Capitol Hill. "It is essential that steps be taken now to preserve an adequate long-range bomber force," the seven said judiciously. "The B-2 remains...the most cost-effective means of rapidly projecting force over great distances."

On numerous occasions during the past decade, Congress seemed all but sure to kill off the B-2. Each time, though, Northrop has managed to fend off the final stake to the heart with a lobbying blitzkrieg, prompting Rep. John Kasich of Ohio to dub the B-2 the "Dracula" bomber. This, then, is how military policy is formulated in the late-20th century: Because a company can mobilize enough lobbying firepower, the American people end up paying for a bomber that doesn't work, to meet a threat that doesn't exist.

CHAPTER SIX

WASHINGTON

ON LESS THAN

$10 MILLION A DAY

A Brief Guide to
Taking Back the Capital

> "Contrary to public opinion, against the public morals, and
> hostile to good government, the lobby has reached such a posi-
> tion of power that it threatens the government itself. Its size,
> its power, its capacity for evil, its greed, trickery, deception and
> fraud condemn it to the death it deserves."
>
> —Hugo Black

To declare that the American political system is desperately
in need of reform is to state the obvious. Providing solutions is
a harder task, especially because in Washington, every call for
reform ends up being blocked or perverted by those who are
content with the status quo: business leaders who know that
the current rules allow them to dominate the political system
by virtue of having the deepest pockets; elected officials who
view public office as an opportunity for self-enrichment; lobbyists who can charge $500 per hour and up to bend the rules for
their clients; PR flacks who get paid similar amounts to manipulate public opinion.

The last time Washington was united in favor of reforming

the political system came in 1974, in the aftermath of the Watergate affair. Following President's Nixon eviction from office, Congress passed laws that were supposed to clean up the campaign finance system. It created the Federal Election Commission, placed strict limits on the amount of money individuals can give to federal candidates ($1,000) or to the national parties ($25,000). The "reform" laws also authorized the creation of Political Action Committees (PACs), which are authorized to give $5,000.

Before long, monied interests found and created loopholes in the system. Big donors escaped the limits by "bundling" $1,000 contributions from business colleagues, family—in some cases donations are made in the name of dependent children—and friends. Most importantly, there are no limits on "soft" money which goes to state organizations, even if that money is spent to benefit a federal candidate. Since Watergate, some 4,000 PACs have been created which funnel hundreds of millions of dollars, most of it from businesses, to candidates during every election cycle. In short, the reforms of 1974 led directly to the "Donorgate" scandals of 1996.

An example more pertinent to this book's main topic involves the beltway's subversion of a lobbying reform law that went into effect in January of 1996. Amid much fanfare and backslapping, the law's supporters claimed that the bill would greatly reduce ties between members of Congress and lobbyists. One provision introduced by the law barred elected officials and their staffers from accepting junket vacations paid for by private interests. A small exception was granted, however: private interests could still pay the way for elected officials to attend "fact-finding" missions or conferences where they were to serve on a panel or as a speaker.

By mid-January, the Tax Foundation put this loophole into practice. It flew ten staffers from the Ways and Means and Finance committees to London, Paris and Rome for a $90,000 "educational" tour on international tax issues. The staffers were accompanied by officials and lobbyists from corporations such as Citicorp, GM, Glaxo and Nestle, the same companies which picked up the cost of the trip. After combing through the new statute, the Tax Foundation determined—and in its infinite wisdom, the Senate Ethics Committee agreed—that since the companies did not pay for the trip directly but funneled their money through the Tax Foundation itself, the excursion did not violate the new law.

One D.C. lobbyist told me that the new rules have in no way cramped his style. "We still arrange trips with members of Congress," he said. "About the only thing that's changed is that I can't pay for extras anymore, like golf course fees."

Another provision of the reform law prohibited House members from accepting any gifts, including meals and entertainment, from lobbyists or other private sources. Senate members could accept freebies worth no more than $100 during the calendar year. A number of popular Capitol Hill eateries were bankrupted by the measure, which reform proponents pointed to as proof that the new law restricts the access lobbyists have to members of Congress.

Once again, though, a loophole in the bill paved the way for further abuses. This one stated that members of Congress could attend free events and excursions sponsored by a national party committee. Very quickly, the parties began arranging weekend fundraising affairs—ski trips to Colorado, Superbowl bashes, etc.—where members attend for free and lobbyists pay for their tickets. As a result, lobbyists can now spend an entire weekend with power brokers, casually discussing their clients' needs and desires, instead of having a rushed conversation about business over lunch.

Thanks to such loopholes, the lobbying reform law produced very little reform. Lobbyists are as powerful as ever and still maintain close financial and social ties with lawmakers.

How, then, can the crooked world of lobbying be cleaned up? There are, obviously, no magical solutions. Indeed, given the flagrant political corruption that currently pervades the political system, it's hard to be optimistic.

Still, there are some hopeful signs, even if they come from around the country and not from Washington itself. The American people know how Washington works and how lobbyists get the job done for their clients. They want the government to cut back on corporate welfare programs and many favor steep reductions in military spending. They are angry about the current state of affairs, as seen in polls that show widespread support for campaign finance reform and for efforts to curtail the power of lobbyists. Public anger is also reflected in the fact that corporations so diligently seek to wrap their lobbying campaigns in "grassroots" packaging in order to win support for their goals.

It's also encouraging that despite massive business spending for lobbying and PR campaigns, the public remains hostile to many of Corporate America's most cherished goals. The American people don't want the government to cozy up to dictatorial regimes such as China, and generally favor putting human rights ahead of commerce in establishing foreign policy. Business groups have spent tens of millions of dollars to convince the public of the virtues of untrammeled "free trade," but big trade agreements such as NAFTA remain deeply unpopular. Corporate America believed that the GOP's takeover of Congress in 1994 would open the way to a rollback of environmental laws, but the rape-and-pillage crowd in Congress had to retreat on many fronts in order to avoid electoral disaster. By 1996, even Newt Gingrich was suggesting that conservatives hold photo-ops at zoos and national parks to demonstrate their devotion to protecting the nation's fauna and flora.

Finally, it's worth noting that attempts to reduce the influence of lobbyists should be seen as just one part of a broader battle to curtail corporate power. Winning better disclosure laws for lobbyists might not sound like a huge triumph, but even a small step like that can help reinvigorate democracy— especially if combined with victories on other fronts, from anti-sweatshop campaigns to campaign finance reform to efforts to protect the environment from corporate plunder.

Here, then, are a few modest suggestions:

Obviously, no reform is possible in isolation. There's no way to reduce the power of lobbyists without first revamping the American system of campaign finance. The cost of running for office is so high—about $500,000 on average to make a run for the House and more than $5 million to run for the Senate— that candidates spend much of their time grubbing for money. Since lobbyists are among the few people in Washington who can afford to attend three to four fundraisers a week at $500 a head, they receive much of the candidates' attention. Howard Marlowe, a past president of the American League for Lobbyists, says politicians and lobbyists have a "mutual addiction": "They need us for money and we need them to help our clients. We don't get access due to our ability or our knowledge of the issues, we get it with money. As a result, we spend way too much time trying to figure out how to buy access."

Marlowe, one of just a few lobbyists who publicly calls for cleaning up the profession, recalled once meeting with a congressional staffer on behalf of a client he represented. Two days later, the same staffer called to invite him to a fundraiser for his boss, and not so subtly reminded him of their earlier meeting. "We need to take the dollar sign out of the legislative process," Marlowe says. "That's the only way that the public will begin again to have faith in the political process."

Second, lobbying disclosure laws need to be far tougher. While the reform bill of 1996 did force greater numbers of lobbyists to register with Congress, it is still riddled with loopholes. As a result, only a fraction of the capital's influence peddlers are required to disclose their activities. Henry Kissinger opens doors for businesses in China (and other countries) and frequently speaks out in favor of improving U.S.-Sino relations. But since he does not directly lobby members of Congress, he is not required to register as a paid agent of Beijing. (It is said that Kissinger's standard contract contains a clause which states that he will do nothing that would require him to register as a lobbyist.)

Disclosure laws must also be brought to bear on so-called "grassroots" lobbyists, who are currently exempted from all reporting requirements. Grassroots lobbying has nothing to do with the First Amendment, as its practitioners shamelessly claim, and everything to do with corporate power.

Bill Hogan of the Center for Public Integrity says that tougher disclosure rules would render lobbyists less powerful. He favors a rule for Congress—which is required for the executive branch—that would force members to keep daily logs of visitors to their offices. "It would be useful if the public knew that lobbyist X had seen Congressman Y twenty times during debate on a bill," Hogan says. "That would be a source of embarrassment to Congressman Y and would reduce such contacts."

Sunshine would help reduce the influence of special interests when it comes to congressional testimony as well. Mark Bloomfield, a top tax lobbyist, frequently testifies before Congress, where he identifies himself as the head of the benignly-named American Council for Capital Formation. A "Truth in Advertising" law for congressional witnesses, as has been proposed by some watchdog groups, would require Bloomfield to also disclose the names of his corporate clients. Such a rule would allow the public to know who's paying for testimony and what interests are behind a given piece of legislation.

Front groups should also be required to be more up front about their membership and funders. The public has a right to know if the "Citizens" involved with Citizens for the Sensible

Control of Acid Rain are electric utilities and coal companies. The Internal Revenue Service doesn't force organizations to report such information on tax forms, but Congress could make full disclosure a requirement for any organization that sends representatives to testify on Capitol Hill.

Perhaps most importantly, something must be done to control the revolving door between the government and "K" Street. President Clinton promised that he would take action on this front, but nothing of consequence was forthcoming. Howard Paster, Clinton's first chief congressional lobbyist, resigned from the powerhouse firm of Hill and Knowlton to work for the president. He lasted less than a year at his post before announcing that he would return to his old firm to serve as chief executive officer.

Public officials can't be permanently barred from lobbying, but they should be prevented from working as influence peddlers for a significant period of time—say five years. That would force them to at least briefly make a respectable living and limit their effectiveness as lobbyists when allowed to again take up the trade. It might also serve as a disincentive to "clock punchers"—those people who come to Washington to learn the ropes and then exploit their knowledge for private gain. One simple step would be to revoke floor access to former members of Congress, a privilege that greatly increases their influence when they become lobbyists.

Perhaps the biggest barrier to reform is that the public's disgust with business-as-usual in Washington has generated far more apathy than it has revolt. That has allowed our elected leaders to talk passionately about the urgent need for change, but take only the most innocuous steps to implement it. Until the public forces the establishment to take action, Washington will remain a place where corporations and lobbyists get their way and ordinary Americans have only the most minimal influence on political decisions.

INDEX

ABOUT THE AUTHOR

Ken Silverstein is co-editor of *CounterPunch*, a Washington, D.C.-based investigative newsletter that *The Village Voice* says "outshines all of its competitors" (For a 1 year subscription, 22 issues, send a check or money order to *CounterPunch*, P.O. Box 18675, Washington, DC 20036). He has written for a number of magazines and newspapers, including *Mother Jones, Harper's* and *The Nation*. Before moving to Washington, Silverstein worked for four years as an *Associated Press* correspondent in Rio de Janeiro, Brazil.